THE COMPLETE GUIDE TO

MANUFACTURED HOUSING

Other books by Gary D. Branson:

The Complete Guide to Floors, Walls, and Ceilings
The Complete Guide to Lumber Yards and Home Centers
The Complete Guide to Recycling at Home
The Complete Guide to Barrier-Free Housing
The Complete Guide to Remodeling Your Basement

THE COMPLETE GUIDE TO

MANUFACTURED HOUSING

The Affordable Alternative to Stick-Built Construction

GARY D. BRANSON

BETTERWAY BOOKS
Cincinnati, Ohio

Acknowledgments

We would like to acknowledge the contributions and cooperation of many members of the manufactured housing industry, without whose help this book would not have been possible. We would like to thank the Manufactured Housing Institute and its Director, Bruce Savage, for information and charts, and for photo contributions, including the cover photo for this book. We also thank Mr. Jack Ireton-Hewitt, President, Burlington Homes of New England; Mr. Jeff Wick, President & COO, Wick Building Systems; and Mr. Walter Wells, President, Schult Homes Corp. We would also like to thank Wausau Homes, Inc. and Miles Homes, Inc. for information and graphic assistance.

Cover photo courtesy of the Manufactured Housing Institute.
Typography by BlackHawk Typesetting

97 96 95 94 93   5 4 3 2 1

Library of Congress Cataloging-in-Publication Data

Branson, Gary D.
    The complete guide to manufactured housing : the affordable
alternative to stick-built construction / Gary D. Branson.
        p. cm.
    Includes index.
      ISBN 1-55870-249-0 : $12.95
    1. Prefabricated houses — Handbooks, manuals, etc. 2. Housing — Handbooks, manuals, etc. I. Title.
TH4819.P7B73 1992
    693'.97 — dc20
                                                                                            92-17904
                                                                                                CIP

Dedicated to Rachel, Michael, and Jacob.

Contents

Introduction

You've seen them in old movies, or, if you are old enough to remember back to the 1950s or beyond, you may have encountered them on the highways. They were called "mobile homes," and they were towed behind cars or trucks, a home away from home, self-contained and eminently portable. Senior citizens towed their mobile homes along for economy in retirement travel, and to follow the sun to escape harsh winters. Itinerant folks, such as salesmen and oil field, agricultural, or construction workers found them to be a solution to their vagabond housing needs as they pursued "sundowner" lifestyles.

This perceived rootless existence of those who dwelt in mobile homes often made the mobile home owner the target of suspicion or disdain in the eyes of his less transient neighbors, and mobile homes and the people who lived in them were often looked down upon. Desi Arnaz and Lucille Ball made a hilarious movie of the pitfalls of vacationing in a mobile home.

But today, manufactured homes have become respectable. As northern "snow birds" discovered warmer southern climes in winter, they often lost their urge to travel and decided to linger awhile, parking their mobile homes on whatever site location they could arrange. In 1955, some enterprising Florida businessman recognized the mobile home owner's urge to linger in one spot, and he established the first mobile home park in the nation, called Trailer Estates, in Bradenton, Florida.

With the mobile homes permanently set up in community parks, people who had found their compact accommodations sufficient when they served merely as a temporary traveling shelter now found them to be needlessly cramped, and they soon demanded more living room. The compact 8-foot wide, 24-foot long mobile homes of those early years grew ever wider and longer. Today, 12-foot and 14-foot wides are common, and 16-foot wide models are available where highway transportation laws permit. Lengths are available up to 76 feet long, and two or more units are often clustered together, so that the homes are equal in total square footage to any expensive stick-built home. When you choose your multi-unit manufactured home today, let your pocketbook be your guide: you can have as much space and as many amenities as you can pay for. The ultimate may be a $300,000.00 model, complete with indoor swimming pool, placed in the luxury park community of Del Tura Country Club in Fort Myers, Florida.

As time passed, the "mobile" feature of mobile homes — a steel frame with axles and wheels — was used only to transport the home to a site, and the homes were permanently placed. Today, 95 percent of all such homes are established on a site and then are never moved again. In fact, because the steel frame underneath the home is a barrier to setting it atop a basement, or to stacking the homes two stories high, there soon will be no steel frames under the homes.

Because "mobile" homes are really no longer mobile, the name was changed. In 1980, the United States Congress stopped using the term "mobile home" and instead began to refer to factory-built housing as "manufactured housing" in all federal laws and publications. Major manufacturers joined together to form a trade association called the Manufactured Housing Institute, located in Arlington, Virginia.

The Manufactured Housing Institute (MHI) works with Congress and regulatory agencies for equitable treatment in housing financing, and publishes statistics related to the manufactured home industry. The institute also works to upgrade construction standards for the industry, and today houses produced by MHI members must meet strict standards for strength, safety, and comfort. Today, each manufactured home sold must exhibit a small red and silver seal, guaranteeing that the home has been inspected and that it meets the federal home construction and safety code, officially called the "National Manufactured Home Construction and Safety Standards."

Some early companies that were involved in mobile home manufacturing were guilty of shabby construction practices, and the homes got a reputation for being substandard and difficult to repair. Today the construction codes and guidelines for manufactured housing are mandated by the Department of Housing and Urban Development (HUD).

For decades, the housing industry has been steadily moving toward use of pre-assembled components to reduce on-site construction time and to reduce labor costs. Today, no matter whether your house is a custom-built mansion or a manufactured home, many or most of the components in the home were assembled in a factory. Windows, doors, cabinets, and roof framing were once assembled or built on site. All are now shipped pre-built, and the on-site builder, like the builder of manufactured housing, has become an assembler.

Manufactured housing just takes off-site assembly one step further: the entire structure is assembled in a factory using fabricated building components, and it is completely finished in temperature-controlled conditions. The economies made possible by factory assembly result in manufactured houses that cost about half as much per square foot as site-built houses. ($24.17 per square foot for multi-section manufactured housing versus $53.25 per square foot for site-built houses, using 1989 industry figures.)

As interest rates moderate, we see in the media that an ever-growing number of families are now finding new housing "affordable." But there is — and for decades has been — a minority of low-income families who simply cannot afford housing costs for site-built housing, no matter how low the interest rates may fall. Statistics show that government regulation and bureaucracy alone may add as much as 20 percent to the cost of site-built homes. During the building boom of the '80s, land prices rose astronomically, pricing many people out of the home market.

Yet another factor spurring the popularity of manufactured housing may be that a growing number of retirees are in the position of: (1) not wanting to maintain a large family home; (2) wishing to spend most or all of their retirement years in warmer parts of the country; (3) wanting the privacy and independence of single-home living rather than apartment living; but (4) seeking affordable — within the limits of retirement incomes — alternatives to site-built housing. Surveys show that people would rather live in manufactured homes than in apartments or condominiums, even if manufactured home living might cost somewhat more. Growing numbers of retirees are finding that manufactured housing offers the affordable option for privacy and for independent living.

Still, building codes and other restrictive barriers remain that make development of manufactured housing difficult or impossible. Many of these codes and restrictions are in fact barely disguised economic or class barriers, clothed in language aimed at barring low-income people from the community, often or usually with the claim that the restrictive legislation is intended to "protect our property values." If contested in court, many or most of these restrictive codes would not stand the test of legality, because they deny our citizens access to affordable housing.

Today, the federal government, via HUD, is moving to remove these restrictions. Jack Kemp, Secretary of HUD, was quoted in the *Manufactured Housing Quarterly* (Fall/Winter 1991) as saying: "Needless rules, red tape and the 'NIMBY' [not in my back yard] syndrome are pushing [housing] prices beyond the reach of most Americans who should be able to afford homes." Kemp goes on: "Housing is one of the most over-regulated industries in this country."

Kemp has endorsed a recent report titled "Not In My Back Yard: Removing Barriers to Affordable Housing," saying: "This report will trigger a significant rethinking of regulations that have put housing almost out of the reach of the poor. We've got to balance between the regulatory process, the tax code, the environment, and the ultimate enemy, which is the 'not in my back yard' syndrome." Further, the report estimates that regulation and exclusionary zoning — combined with pure bureaucracy — may add as much as 20 to 35 percent to housing prices. Many local housing restrictions have been enacted by city councils or other minor government officials who have no legal training, and their restrictions have never been tested in the courts.

Surely all citizens would endorse and support any reasonable regulations that actually contribute to better housing values or to increased home safety. But there are few people in the housing industry who would argue with Secretary Jack Kemp's assertion that "Housing is one of the most over-regulated industries in this country." I have seen instances where a builder was required to install a gas chimney in an all-electric house, because the code calling for a chimney was written when only combustion (gas or oil) furnaces were available, before electric radiant heating was developed. For years, the plastering unions fought the advances of use of drywall or wallboard in homes and apartment dwellings, and these local restrictions were struck down only when drywall contractors sued the cities for discrimination.

We need to review our housing codes and to identify those codes that do not serve us well. Old codes that regulate the size of the house that can be built, or mandate the type of water pipes used only to protect union workers' jobs, should be reviewed. These expensive and exclusionary codes and restrictive policies must be reviewed and/or removed if we are to house our nation.

1
The Manufactured Housing Industry

There are about eighty-five companies building manufactured homes in over 230 factories in the U.S. There is a network of between 5,500 and 6,000 dealers selling the homes. In 1989, nearly 25 percent of all homes sold were manufactured homes. The value of manufactured homes sold in 1989 totaled about $5.3 billion.

In the old days, the term "mobile homes" conjured up a vision of cheap construction with lots of flimsy, pre-finished paneling. Today's manufactured houses are built to strict industry standards to meet national building codes.

WHY THE TIMES HAVE CHANGED

In the past, all stick-built houses were built board by board on site. Windows were assembled from their many component pieces; doors and frames were assembled, hung on hinges, lock holes bored, and locks installed. Cabinets were built on site: table saws and planers were hauled into the house, and each piece of cabinetry and trim was cut and shaped by the carpenters. This type of residential construction became the standard for "quality," and any deviation from this procedure was looked down upon by tradesmen as somehow of lesser quality. Any builder who is old enough to remember the 1950s will remember that real carpenters looked with disdain upon such newfangled developments as pre-hung doors and pre-finished cabinetry. At the same time, the consumer continued to look upon builders who used such new components as some-how less than quality builders. The entire building industry understood that to be quality, house components had to be built on the job.

Controlling Costs with Pre-Assembly

But the one thing you can count on is that the housing market is capital driven, meaning the dollar is king. As labor and other costs rose, there was a continuing search for ways to compete financially, and one of the ways to control costs was to use pre-assembled components. So we slowly began to see roof trusses, wall panels, pre-hung doors, pre-finished cabinetry, siding, and paneling being used in new houses. Carpenters and other tradesmen became assemblers rather than craftsmen.

The manufactured housing industry takes the trend toward building componentization one step further: they build the entire house in a factory, using components that are not only pre-assembled but are also pre-finished. This reduces the on-site labor: little painting is required at the assembly site, because the pieces are all finished at the factory of origin.

ADVANTAGES OF FACTORY ASSEMBLY

Weather

Advantages of factory assembly include overcoming the one greatest foe for the site builder: the weather. No matter how organized the builder is, the weather can cause endless delays, plus problems with job quality. Freezing weather can delay excavation, concrete work, painting, and wallboard finishing. For example, serious quality problems may result if drying of wallboard finishing compounds is delayed. Once the wallboard compound is in place, quality demands that the compound dry as quickly as possible. If drying is delayed, moisture can soak into the edges of wallboard panels, causing unsightly ridging of the seams between panels. The wet compound can also cause wallboard screws or nails to rust, and the rust may bleed through finish coats of paint.

Other Effects on Construction

Site painting not only suffers from such weather conditions as moisture and temperature extremes, but also can be affected by blown dust and dirt caused by other construction trades. Quality control is enhanced in a factory because even minor problems one might encounter at the job site are eliminated by factory assembly. One minor example: Well water or other extremely hard water found in local communities can affect paint color when used to thin paint. Water quality and tool cleanliness can be controlled more easily under factory conditions.

CONSTRUCTION CODES

Since 1976, all manufactured homes must meet guidelines established by Congress in the National Manufactured Home Construction and Safety Standards. Administered by the Department of Housing and Urban Development (HUD), these codes make manufactured housing the only segment of the housing industry that is governed by a national building code. The code regulates the construction, design, strength, energy efficiency, and fire resistance of manufactured housing, as well as monitoring the installation of the mechanical equipment for heating, air conditioning, electrical service, and plumbing.

Handling Complaints

HUD also manages a national complaint department for consumers who buy manufactured hous-

ing. The initial consumer complaint is heard by state administrative agencies in thirty-five states and by the National Conference of States on Building Codes and Standards in the other fifteen states. This national complaint system is not a part of the manufacturers' warranties, but is in addition to those warranties. HUD also has authority to demand repairs of major defects or any imminent safety hazard for the life of the manufactured house. The consumer may take any complaint all the way to the national HUD office, and HUD monitors all customer complaints to see if there is a pattern of problems that should be addressed in the industry. This monitoring of problems permits the industry to adjust building codes and procedures to eliminate complaints and callbacks.

ECONOMIC ADVANTAGES

Other economies and use of better building materials are possible through quantity buying and total mechanization. Factory building permits use of the latest power tools, including air-driven nailers, staplers, and sanders. Workers can be trained to perform certain assigned tasks at one work station, so they become more proficient at their jobs. Also, panels are built flat on platforms and then tipped up in place, eliminating the need for much unproductive scaffold building and moving. A great deal of effort is wasted on traditional job sites, just in building and climbing scaffolding. As these and other labor-saving procedures are followed in home factories, the basic cost of building is reduced. The manufactured housing industry produces multi-section houses (two manufactured housing units joined together to form one house) at a cost about one-half the cost of site-built housing.

Compare the Costs

For example, in 1990, the average square footage of the multi-section manufactured house was 1,440 square feet, at an average sales price of $36,600.00, or $25.42 per square foot. This cost, of course, does not reflect land prices for siting of the manufactured house, because the unit may be sited on a private lot, or may be placed in a community development where a monthly rental fee may be paid for the site. Multi-section homes accounted for about 48 percent of sales of manufactured housing. Single-section homes averaged 980 square feet, costing $19,800.00 for a cost per square foot of $20.20.

By contrast, the site-built house contained an average of 2,050 square feet and cost an average of $149,800.00, including an average land or lot cost of $41,048.00. When the lot cost is subtracted from the total, the actual cost of the structure itself was $108,752.00, and the cost of the structure was more than double the cost of a manufactured house at $53.05 per square foot.

Affordability Sells Homes

Surveys of owners of manufactured homes state that a primary reason for purchase of their homes is affordability. Manufactured homes not only cost less per square foot than site-built homes, they also offer the advantage of being partially or totally furnished from the factory, so little or no investment is needed for furnishings.

TYPES OF FACTORY-BUILT HOMES

In addition to building the homes that were previously called "mobile homes," the factory-built housing industry also builds *panelized homes, pre-cut homes, modular homes* and *log* or *timber homes.*

Panelized Homes

Panelized homes are homes built panel by panel (or wall by wall) in the factory. Each wall or ceiling panel may be complete, including electrical wiring, insulation, inside wallboard, and outside siding. (Some panels do not include either interior or exterior finishes.) The appropriate number of panels are transported to the building site and are there assembled to build the house. Panelized homes are usually erected by professionals, using cranes to lift and fit the panels into place.

Pre-Cut Homes

Pre-cut homes mean that the building materials are pre-cut to fit at the factory, then bundled together into kits and shipped to the site for assembly. In effect, with pre-cut homes you are buying a lumber pile, but the mathematics of measuring and cutting are done for you, and all you have to do is to nail the pieces together at the site. Examples of pre-cut homes include kit, log, and dome homes.

In this book, when we refer to manufactured homes or factory-built homes, we refer only to those houses that are *completely* built at the factory. This means only manufactured homes and modular homes. All other types of "manufactured" housing — panelized, pre-cut, and log or timber homes — require significant assembly work at the site. In addition, specialty homes such as log or timber homes, while beautiful homes, require special assembly skills and are significantly higher in price than other types of manufactured housing.

THE POSITION OF THE MANUFACTURED HOUSING INSTITUTE

The Manufactured Housing Institute (MHI) represents only manufactured and modular housing — housing that is completely built in a factory and is delivered as a finished product, just as your auto is delivered as a finished product from the factory. The MHI has dedicated its industry to housing the 20 percent or more of families who cannot afford more expensive site-built housing.

Following is the stated goal of the Manufactured Housing Institute.

By [the year] 2000 the manufactured housing industry should:

- capture 51 percent of the single-family market;
- enjoy consumer regard for its advantages and benefits;
- be accepted as part of the housing industry at all levels;
- have parity in zoning and financing with site-built homes;
- be recognized as ethical and professional;
- have unanimity of direction, purpose, and goals.

2
Who Buys Manufactured Homes?

In the decade of the 1980s, almost one-third (29.8 percent) of all new homes sold were manufactured homes. Today, there are about 7.1 million manufactured homes in the nation, housing 12.9 million people.

RESULTS OF A SURVEY

A survey of 24,000 manufactured home households, conducted by the Marketing Research Department of the Foremost Insurance Company and titled "Manufactured Homes: The Market Facts," has given us a working profile of manufactured home owners. The largest segment of ownership is blue collar at 35 percent, with white collar people owning 24 percent, retired people 26 percent, and "other" owning 15 percent of the manufactured homes.

By age of head of household, 10 percent were under 30; 25 percent were thirty to thirty-nine, 18 percent were forty to forty-nine, and 13 percent were between fifty and fifty-nine years of age. The average age of manufactured home owners rose slightly to fifty years; 34 percent of owners were over sixty years of age.

New Buyers
But the profile for *new buyers* is changing when it is compared to the profile for *present owners*. Considered by income, 32 percent of manufactured homes are bought by people earning $10,000-$19,999; another 32 percent are bought by people earning $20,000-$29,999; 18 percent of buyers earn $30,000-$39,999; 9 percent earn over $40,000 per year, and 9 percent earn under $10,000 per year.

Although manufactured homes are often the first-time buyer choice of the young, who may have limited income, the survey figures show that 27 percent of buyers earn more than $30,000.00 per year and 29 percent are "empty nesters" who are over fifty years of age. There has been a rapid growth of manufactured housing communities for the retired in the warmer climes, such as Florida and Nevada.

The Image vs. the Reality
One critical image of those who live in manufactured homes has been that of a transient family with a house full of children, running undisciplined and overloading school facilities. The latest survey shows that particular image was *never* true: in 1981, 60 percent of manufactured home families consisted of only one or two people; 91 percent had four members or fewer. In 1990, 63 percent of manufactured home families consisted of one or two people, and 93 percent of families had four members or less. In fact, 58 percent of manufactured home families consisted of a married couple; 9 percent of homes housed a single male; and 19 percent housed a single female. That means that a full 86 percent of manufactured home households consist of either a single person or a married couple.

No "Typical" Owner

The Manufactured Housing Institute states that industry studies show "there is no 'typical owner.' Owners come from all walks of life and nearly half previously owned a site-built home.

"The profile of new buyers has changed since the previous survey in 1984. They are older — 41.6 years of age compared to 38.2; fewer are blue collar workers — 35 percent compared to 42 percent; they have higher median incomes — $21,900 compared to $19,700. The number of new buyers making $30,000 or more a year has increased by half, to 18 percent, since 1984."

MANUFACTURED HOME BUYERS BY REGION

Manufactured home sales are, to varying degrees, affected by discriminatory practices and codes in various cities and regions, and the department of Housing and Urban Development (HUD) is trying to tear down unfair or artificial barriers to manufactured housing. Patterns for buying manufactured housing will change as restrictive codes are removed and consumers can make more democratic choices in where and how they will live.

Manufactured home sales today are highest in warmer climates. The top ten states for manufactured home sales are: Florida, North Carolina, Georgia, South Carolina, Texas, Alabama, Michigan, Tennessee, Washington, and California.

AN ATTRACTIVE OPTION FOR MANY

For Senior Citizens

As we have mentioned, for senior citizens, manufactured housing has increasingly become an attractive and affordable alternative to site-built housing. Seniors prefer manufactured homes for their low maintenance, convenient living, and affordability. Owning a manufactured home lets you enjoy privacy and independent living, and it costs less than renting a house or an apartment. Median housing costs per month (American Housing Survey, quoted by the MHI) are $253.00 for manufac-

tured homes, $399.00 for home and apartment renters, and $375.00 for all homeowners.

As Second Homes

Manufactured homes also are popular for use as second homes in remote recreational areas such as lake or seashore retreats. In small towns where trained and competitive building crews are unavailable, the manufactured home is often an affordable and available option. Where two or more generations of a family share a farmstead, manufactured homes can provide temporary or permanent housing for young families or retirement living for older generations. Manufactured housing has also long been a choice of migrant construction or other workers, who move to be near major construction projects or the latest well drilled in a newly developed "oil patch."

Housing in Rural Areas

Rural states, particularly the rural south, have seen a rapid growth in the sale of manufactured homes. Rural areas, including small towns, have fewer trained construction crews, have fewer contractors to make competitive bids on each job, and are not located near low-cost suppliers of building materials. Also, income levels in rural areas are below the higher-paid urban areas where competition for workers boosts labor rates. The economy of manufactured home prices makes them an attractive housing choice in rural areas for all these reasons.

But rural or recreational applications are by no means the main thrust of the manufactured home industry. By a margin of 93 percent, the majority of manufactured homes are owned by working people who live in or near major cities and job centers. Ownership of manufactured housing today is largely dependent on the development of community parks that can accommodate the homes.

THE NEWEST COMMUNITY PARKS

Manufactured housing communities have come a long way since the first "mobile home" park, Trailer Estates, was established in Bradenton, Florida in

1955. Copying that initial effort, trailer parks sprouted across the nation; crowded spaces where mobile homes were packed tightly together in a converted corn field, with no trees or landscaping to provide eye appeal or shelter from the blazing sun or wintry gales. There were no carports or garages for cars or for storage, and toys, abandoned cars, and unused furniture often cluttered the landscape. A large percentage of housing industry professionals — builders, real estate agents, mortgage brokers, and bankers — had a negative attitude toward these unwanted neighbors.

It was a Catch-22: communities looked down upon their then-unattractive neighbors and passed local ordinances and codes designed to bar or discourage park developments. Today, in increasing numbers of cities, developers are building manufactured home communities that are well-planned and attractive additions to their areas. The homes are sited on larger lots; have paved driveways, carports, or garages; and are landscaped to match developments for site-built houses. As the design and development of manufactured home sites improves, so too do community attitudes.

An example of this upgrade in development, cited in the Fall/Winter 1991 issue of *Manufactured Housing Quarterly* (*MHQ*) is Shelby Forest, a suburb of Detroit, Michigan. In addition to good planning and landscaping, the development has a club house and swimming pool. All the manufactured homes in the development have pitched, shingled roofs and house-type siding. The 625-space, landlease housing community was filled quickly, and a new development, Shelby West, was built.

Higher Appreciation Rates

So successful have planned manufactured home communities become that the old premise of high depreciation for such homes is no longer true. (The industry calls this attitude a myth and states that it was never true.) A study done by the California Manufactured Housing Institute (CMHI) showed that, in three out of four communities, manufac-

tured home values increased faster than did site-built home values in the same areas. In Jackson Heights Estates (El Cajon), Stonegate Ventura, and Green Hills (Yorba Linda), manufactured homes appreciated at rates higher than site-built homes. A study in the state of Washington showed similar results in six counties surveyed.

High Levels of Satisfaction

The survey shows that 87 percent of owners queried state that they are very satisfied (53 percent) or somewhat satisfied (34 percent) with manufactured home living. One-fourth or 25 percent of manufactured home dwellers plan to move in less than five years, but 57 percent intend to stay "always" in their current homes, and 18 percent think they will stay put for at least five years, possibly more.

REASONS FOR PURCHASING A MANUFACTURED HOME

A high percentage of manufactured home buyers — 78 percent — listed price advantages as one of the main reasons they bought the home, and another 38 percent cited the further savings of buying a home that was already substantially furnished. Other reasons cited (by 19 percent of respondents) include the possibility of relocating the manufactured home (although 95 percent of homes are never moved from their initial site); the elderly or less able (13 percent) like the fact that there are no steps and the home is all on one level; some purchased the unit as a retirement home (15 percent) or a vacation home (1 percent); some buyers (13 percent) liked the quality of construction; some buyers (43 percent) liked the idea of owning their own land or paying a small monthly parking rental. Some 61 percent of owners like the idea of owning their own home versus renting, 26 percent cite the convenient location of their manufactured home, 34 percent liked the interior design or floor plan of their choice, 13 percent liked the manufacturer's warranty, and 10 percent said they bought a manufactured home on the advice of a friend or relative.

ADVANTAGES OF MANUFACTURED HOME LIVING

Now that they own manufactured homes, what advantages cause owners to stay in the homes? The most common reason given, by 69 percent, is affordability. Other advantages mentioned include easy housekeeping/yard work, 44 percent; lower utility costs, 42 percent; mobility, 19 percent (although again, 95 percent of manufactured homes are never moved from their first site, and in this particular survey only 7 percent *had* moved their manufactured home in the past three years); lower taxes, 45 percent; low park rent, 17 percent; privacy, 39 percent; less maintenance on the home, 35 percent; having neighbors close by, 25 percent; well-utilized space, 38 percent; and pride of ownership, 58 percent.

How can we weigh owner satisfaction with manufactured homes? Consider the length of ownership: 18 percent have lived in their manufactured homes for less than five years; 69 percent have lived in their homes for five to nineteen years, and 13 percent have lived in a manufactured home for twenty years or more. These figures seem to indicate a high level of satisfaction on the part of manufactured home dwellers. But what are the disadvantages?

DISADVANTAGES OF MANUFACTURED HOME LIVING

The Foremost Insurance survey listed the disadvantages cited by manufactured home dwellers. At the top of the list was the small size and lack of storage space, cited by 46 percent, and, in the same vein, 58 percent listed lack of a basement, a garage, or an attic as a disadvantage. Others — 43 percent — listed the danger of fire or storm damage. Almost half — 45 percent — listed high depreciation, although industry studies dispute this factor, citing studies done by the California Manufactured Housing Association that show manufactured housing appreciating at a rate above or comparable to that of site-built housing, assuming the manufactured home is located in a well-planned community park.

Other disadvantages of manufactured home living include: park rental fees that continually escalate, 26 percent; difficulty of resale of the home, 18 percent; difficulty of repair or faulty construction by 20 percent; high heating/cooling costs by 25 percent (see Chapter 4, Choosing a Home Site); dissatisfaction with the park owner or manager, 21 percent; and other people's opinions of manufactured home owners, 14 percent.

CONCLUSION

The lists of advantages and disadvantages from manufactured home owners should serve as a good buying guide to anyone considering buying a manufactured home. All the advantages cited should provide points of comparison for the prospective manufactured home buyer.

The Foremost Insurance survey, "Manufactured Homes: The Market Facts," was conducted by their Marketing Research Department for the Michigan Manufactured Housing Association and for the national Manufactured Housing Institute. Although the survey was intended to serve the manufactured housing industry, it is a useful guide for the prospective buyer as well. To avoid future disappointments, it would be wise for the consumer to study both the advantages and disadvantages of manufactured home living.

Studying the list of disadvantages cited in the survey reveals that many or most of those problems listed could be avoided by more careful and thoughtful shopping, both in reference to the home itself and to the home site. Buying the wrong home, or siting it in the wrong park/area, can be disastrous for any home buyer, whether buying a site-built or manufactured home.

A review of those listed disadvantages reveals problems with owners or managers of manufactured home parks. You should be able to avoid these problems by making a drive-through of the home park and checking manager housekeeping: 6 percent of the survey respondents simply did not like the park owner/manager, 8 percent cited poor maintenance by the owner/manager, and 7 percent did not like renter restrictions mandated by the owner/manager. You should ask for a written list of park restrictions before signing a lease; checking with other neighboring park dwellers should reveal whether the park's owner/manager is disagreeable or unreasonable.

Make a Considered Decision

Consider the advantages and disadvantages of manufactured home living before making a buying decision. Keep in mind that not all of us would see "advantages" in the same way: having neighbors nearby might be seen as an advantage by the gregarious, but would be considered a disadvantage by the less sociable among us. Would you see the advantages listed in the survey as advantages that you would endorse or enjoy? How about the disadvantages?

Many of the disadvantages listed relate only to homes that have been sited in community parks: noisy neighbors, rising monthly rental fees, conflict with park owners/managers, and fear that the park may be sold can be avoided by shopping more carefully for your rental home site or by buying your own lot. Can you avoid or minimize the disadvantages listed, perhaps by siting the home on your own land? Study Chapter 4, Choosing a Home Site, carefully to be sure you make the right decisions.

SHIPMENTS OF MANUFACTURED HOMES BY STATE
Ranked from Highest to Lowest
January 1992

State	Total Shipment	% of Total	Rank	Single Sectn. Shpmnt	% of Total	Rank	Multi Sectn. Shpmnt	% of Total	Rank
Florida	1,422	11.1%	1	486	7.4%	2	936	15.2%	1
North Carolina	1,268	9.9%	2	741	11.2%	1	527	8.5%	2
Georgia	777	6.1%	3	388	5.9%	3	389	6.3%	3
South Carolina	673	5.3%	4	385	5.8%	4	288	4.7%	8
Texas	617	4.8%	5	332	5.0%	7	285	4.6%	9
Alabama	556	4.4%	6	379	5.7%	5	177	2.9%	10
Michigan	527	4.1%	7	221	3.3%	12	306	5.0%	7
Tennessee	505	4.0%	8	354	5.4%	6	151	2.4%	12
Washington	456	3.6%	9	84	1.3%	23	372	6.0%	5
California	430	3.4%	10	52	0.8%	28	378	6.1%	4
Kentucky	403	3.2%	11	302	4.6%	8	101	1.6%	19
Oregon	391	3.1%	12	44	0.7%	31	347	5.6%	6
Pennsylvania	387	3.0%	13	238	3.6%	9	149	2.4%	13
Virginia	362	2.8%	14	219	3.3%	13	143	2.3%	15
Indiana	351	2.7%	15	207	3.1%	14	144	2.3%	14
Ohio	341	2.7%	16	223	3.4%	11	118	1.9%	17
Mississippi	313	2.5%	17	226	3.4%	10	87	1.4%	20
New York	307	2.4%	18	171	2.6%	17	136	2.2%	16
Missouri	256	2.0%	19	170	2.6%	18	86	1.4%	21
Arkansas	251	2.0%	20	176	2.7%	16	75	1.2%	22
Arizona	248	1.9%	21	79	1.2%	25	169	2.7%	11
Louisiana	218	1.7%	22	179	2.7%	15	39	0.6%	28
West Virginia	205	1.6%	23	133	2.0%	19	72	1.2%	25
New Mexico	177	1.4%	24	102	1.5%	20	75	1.2%	23
Illinois	147	1.2%	25	87	1.3%	22	60	1.0%	26
Kansas	141	1.1%	26	89	1.3%	21	52	0.8%	27
Nevada	127	1.0%	27	22	0.3%	36	105	1.7%	18
Idaho	119	0.9%	28	45	0.7%	30	74	1.2%	24
Iowa	109	0.9%	29	84	1.3%	24	25	0.4%	32
Wisconsin	93	0.7%	30	73	1.1%	26	20	0.3%	40
Maine	88	0.7%	31	66	1.0%	27	22	0.4%	38
Oklahoma	82	0.6%	32	48	0.7%	29	34	0.6%	29
Colorado	53	0.4%	33	23	0.3%	35	30	0.5%	30
Delaware	52	0.4%	34	27	0.4%	33	25	0.4%	34
Minnesota	50	0.4%	35	24	0.4%	34	26	0.4%	31
Maryland	49	0.4%	36	27	0.4%	32	22	0.4%	39
Montana	46	0.4%	37	21	0.3%	37	25	0.4%	33
South Dakota	45	0.4%	38	20	0.3%	38	25	0.4%	35
Nebraska	39	0.3%	39	16	0.2%	39	23	0.4%	37
Utah	28	0.2%	40	4	0.1%	44	24	0.4%	36
Vermont	21	0.2%	41	14	0.2%	40	7	0.1%	42
New Jersey	14	0.1%	42	4	0.1%	42	10	0.2%	41
Connecticut	9	0.1%	43	4	0.1%	43	5	0.1%	43
New Hampshire	8	0.1%	44	7	0.1%	41	1	0.0%	48
North Dakota	6	0.0%	45	2	0.0%	45	4	0.1%	44
Massachusetts	4	0.0%	46	2	0.0%	46	2	0.0%	46
Wyoming	2	0.0%	47	0	0.0%	47	2	0.0%	45
Rhode Island	1	0.0%	48	0	0.0%	49	1	0.0%	47
Hawaii	0	0.0%	49	0	0.0	48	0	0.0%	50
Alaska	0	0.0%	50	0	0.0%	50	0	0.0%	49
	12,774	100.2%		6,600	99.8		6,174	99.9%	

Does Not Include Destination Pending (Beginning Inventory)
Percentages May Not Add to 100% Because of Rounding
Courtesy of the Manufactured Housing Institute.

1990 CENSUS DATA

State	Existing Manuf. Homes as of Year End 1990	Total Structures as of Year End 1990	Manuf. Homes as a Percent of Total Structures
Alabama	224,307	1,670,379	13.43%
Alaska	20,280	232,608	8.72%
Arizona	250,597	1,659,430	15.10%
Arkansas	131,542	1,000,667	13.15%
California	555,307	11,182,882	4.97%
Colorado	88,683	1,477,349	6.00%
Connecticut	12,118	1,320,850	0.92%
Delaware	34,944	289,919	12.05%
Washington D.C.	82	278,489	0.03%
Florida	762,855	6,100,262	12.51%
Georgia	305,055	2,638,418	11.56%
Hawaii	389	389,810	0.10%
Idaho	56,529	413,327	13.68%
Illinois	150,733	4,506,275	3.34%
Indiana	156,821	2,246,046	6.98%
Iowa	56,857	1,143,669	4.97%
Kansas	71,195	1,044,112	6.82%
Kentucky	185,336	1,506,845	12.30%
Louisiana	196,236	1,716,241	11.43%
Maine	54,532	587,045	9.29%
Maryland	42,729	1,891,917	2.26%
Massachusetts	23,928	2,472,711	0.97%
Michigan	246,365	3,847,926	6.40%
Minnesota	90,864	1,848,445	4.92%
Mississippi	136,948	1,010,423	13.55%
Missouri	164,021	2,199,129	7.46%
Montana	54,021	361,155	14.96%
Nebraska	37,046	660,621	5.61%
Nevada	69,655	518,858	13.42%
New Hampshire	35,334	503,904	7.01%
New Jersey	33,551	3,075,310	1.09%
New Mexico	102,948	632,058	16.29%
New York	194,934	7,226,891	2.70%
North Carolina	430,440	2,818,193	15.27%
North Dakota	27,055	276,340	9.79%
Ohio	205,595	4,371,945	4.70%
Oklahoma	129,850	1,406,499	9.23%
Oregon	134,325	1,193,567	11.25%
Pennsylvania	254,920	4,938,140	5.16%
Rhode Island	4,689	414,572	1.13%
South Carolina	240,525	1,424,155	16.89%
South Dakota	31,357	292,436	10.72%
Tennessee	188,517	2,026,067	9.30%
Texas	547,911	7,008,999	7.82%
Utah	34,986	598,388	5.85%
Vermont	22,702	271,214	8.37%
Virginia	159,352	2,496,334	6.38%
Washington	187,533	2,032,378	9.23%
West Virginia	118,733	781,295	15.20%
Wisconsin	101,149	2,055,774	4.92%
Wyoming	33,474	203,411	16.46%
TOTALS	7,399,855	102,263,678	7.24%

Courtesy of the Manufactured Housing Institute.

MARKET DATA USERS' SERVICE
NATIONWIDE REPORT

I. DEMOGRAPHIC INFORMATION

	1981	1984	1987	1990
Age of Household Head				
Less than 30 Years	24%	21%	20%	10%
30-39 Years	25%	23%	25%	25%
40-49 Years	10%	12%	14%	18%
50-59 Years	13%	12%	11%	13%
60-69 Years	15%	17%	15%	18%
70 Years and Over	13%	16%	15%	17%
Total Percentage	100%	100%	100%	100%
Number Responding	6,968	7,276	16,568	15,401
Average Age	46	47	47	50
Employment Status of Household Head				
Full Time	64%	59%	59%	60%
Part Time	6%	6%	7%	7%
Retired	23%	26%	26%	27%
Not Employed	8%	9%	8%	6%
Total Percentage	101%	100%	100%	100%
Number Responding	6,965	7,276	16,391	15,053
Occupation of Household Head				
Retired	23%	26%	26%	26%
Operator/Laborer	20%	20%	18%	15%
Tech/Sales/Admin Support	15%	12%	12%	10%
Craftsman/Repairman	12%	12%	11%	13%
Managerial/Professional	9%	10%	8%	12%
Service	8%	8%	7%	8%
Student/Armed Forces/Other	8%	9%	15%	13%
Farming/Forestry/Fishing	4%	4%	3%	2%
Total Percentage	99%	101%	100%	99%
Number Responding	6,968	7,276	16,432	15,401
Education of Household Head				
Attended Grade School	3%	3%	3%	3%
Grade School Graduate	6%	5%	6%	5%
Attended High School	14%	16%	16%	15%
High School Graduate	44%	43%	44%	42%
Attended College	20%	22%	22%	25%
College Graduate	7%	6%	5%	6%
College Post Graduate	5%	5%	4%	4%
Total Percentage	99%	100%	100%	100%
Number Responding	6,959	7,265	16,535	15,337
Marital Status				
Now Married	65%	66%	62%	58%
Never Married	13%	9%	9%	10%
Divorced/Widowed/Separated	22%	25%	29%	32%
Total Percentage	100%	100%	100%	100%
Number Responding	6,968	7,276	16,567	15,401

Courtesy Foremost Insurance Co.

MARKET DATA USERS' SERVICE
NATIONWIDE REPORT
(cont.)

	1981	1984	1987	1990
Annual Household Income				
Less than $10,000	29%	27%	23%	18%
$10,000 - $19,999	41%	37%	35%	32%
$20,000 - $29,999	23%	22%	24%	26%
$30,000 - $39,999	5%	9%	12%	14%
$40,000 and Over	2%	5%	7%	10%
Total Percentage	100%	100%	101%	100%
Number Responding	6,968	7,276	16,568	15,401
Median Income Level	$14,500	$16,000	$17,500	$20,100
Total Net Worth				
Less than $50,000				55%
$50,000 - $99,999				27%
$100,000 - $249,999				13%
$250,000 - $499,999				3%
$500,000 - $999,999				1%
$1,000,000 and Over				0%
Total Percentage				99%
Number Responding				14,340
Median Net Worth				$45,000
Household Size				
1 Member	25%	23%	24%	27%
2 Members	35%	37%	34%	36%
3 Members	16%	18%	18%	16%
4 Members	15%	15%	15%	14%
5 or More Members	8%	7%	8%	7%
Total Percentage	99%	100%	99%	100%
Number Responding	6,968	7,276	16,568	15,401
Average Household Size	2.5	2.5	2.5	2.4
RMA Population Densities				
Less than 50,000	50%	58%	58%	57%
50,000 - 499,999	21%	19%	21%	20%
500,000 - 1,999,999	20%	12%	11%	10%
2,000,000 and Over	9%	11%	10%	13%
Total Percentage	100%	100%	100%	100%
Number Responding	6,968	7,276	16,568	15,401
Family Household Designation				
Husband and Wife	65%	66%	62%	58%
Male and Child/Other Relative	0%	1%	1%	2%
Female and Child/Other Relative	6%	9%	10%	10%
Male Living Alone	7%	5%	6%	9%
Female Living Alone	19%	18%	18%	19%
Male and Non-Relative	1%	0%	1%	1%
Female and Non-Relative	2%	1%	2%	2%
Total Percentage	100%	100%	100%	101%
Number Responding	6,968	7,276	16,568	15,401

Courtesy Foremost Insurance Co.

MARKET DATA USERS' SERVICE
NATIONWIDE REPORT
(cont.)

II. OPINIONS AND LIFE-STYLE OF MOBILE HOME OWNERS

	1981	1984	1987	1990
Satisfaction with MH Living				
Very Satisfied	59%	58%	52	53%
Somewhat Satisfied	31%	31%	35%	34%
Somewhat Dissatisfied	7%	8%	9%	9%
Very Dissatisfied	3%	3%	4%	4%
Total Percentage	100%	100%	100%	100%
Number Responding	6,923	7,153	16,403	15,150
Other Housing Types Considered at Time of MH Purchase				
Site-Built House				32%
Apartment/Townhouse				16%
Condominium				5%
Other				2%
None Others Considered				53%
Number Responding*				14,904
Reasons for Purchasing a MH Instead of Another Housing Type				
Less Expensive to Buy				78%
Instant Housing/Furnished				38%
Mobility/Can Relocate MH				19%
No Steps/All on One Level				13%
Purchased for a Vacation Home				1%
Purchased for a Retirement Home				15%
Quality Construction in a MH				13%
Could Own Land				21%
Low Monthly Park Rent				22%
Wanted to Own Home Instead of Rent				61%
Convenient Location Available for a MH				26%
Liked the Floor Plan/Interior Design/Decor				34%
MH Included a Manufacturer's Warranty				13%
A Friend/Relative Recommended MH Living				10%
Other				13%
Number Responding*				14,879
MH Living Advantages that Cause Them to Remain in a MH				
Easy to Keep Clean/Less Yard Work				44%
Less Expensive to Heat/Keep Cool				42%
Mobility/Can Relocate MH				19%
Taxes are Lower				45%
Low Monthly Park Rent				17%
It's Private/Quiet				39%
Can Afford to Live in a MH				69%
Less Maintenance Required Inside/Outside a MH				45%
Like the Activities Available in a MH Park				8%
Like Having Neighbors Watch Out for Each Other				25%
Less Expensive to Maintain/Repair a MH				35%
Space is Well Utilized/Compact/Cozy				38%
I Have the Pride of Ownership—It's All Mine				58%
Other				5%
Number Responding*				14,938

*The percentage totals over 100% due to multiple responses.
Courtesy Foremost Insurance Co.

MARKET DATA USERS' SERVICE
NATIONWIDE REPORT
(cont.)

	1981	1984	1987	1990
Major Disadvantages of MH Living				
Too Small/No Storage Space				46%
Fire/Storm Danger				43%
No Basement/Garage/Attic				58%
Depreciates Quickly				45%
Park Rental Fees Keep Increasing				26%
Neighbors are Too Noisy/No Privacy				8%
Difficult to Sell Our MH				18%
Fear that MH Park Will Be Sold				8%
Poor Construction/Difficult to Repair				20%
Difficult to Heat/Cool/Poorly Insulated				25%
Don't Like Our Park Manager/Owner				6%
Poor Maintenance by Park Manager/Owner				8%
Don't Like the Restrictions in Our MH Park				7%
Other People's Opinions of MH Owners				14%
Other				4%
No Major Disadvantages				9%
Number Responding*				15,188
Percentage Having Redecorated Their MH Within Last Three Years				58%
Number Responding				15,058
Percentage Having Added Landscaping Features Within Last Three Years				64%
Number Responding				15,114
MH Residence Usage				
Own—Use as Primary Residence				93%
Own—Use as Vacation/Winter Home				1%
Own—Rent Out to Others				1%
Rent from Owners				6%
Total Percentage				101%
Number Responding				15,355
Percentage Stating MH Has Been Moved in Last Three Years				7%
Number Responding				15,231
Years Ever Owned/Lived in a MH				
Less than 5 Years	34%	27%	27%	18%
5-9 Years	36%	35%	32%	30%
10-19 Years	26%	32%	34%	39%
20 Years or More	4%	6%	8%	13%
Total Percentage	100%	100%	101%	100%
Number Responding	6,885	7,238	16,398	15,304
Median Years in a MH		7	8	10

*The percentage totals over 100% due to multiple responses.

Courtesy Foremost Insurance Co.

MARKET DATA USERS' SERVICE
NATIONWIDE REPORT
(cont.)

	1981	1984	1987	1990
Additional Years Planning to Own/Live in Current MH				
Less than 5 Years	30%	31%	30%	25%
5 Years or More	20%	16%	19%	18%
Always	50%	53%	51%	57%
Total Percentage	100%	100%	100%	100%
Number Responding	6,322	6,903	15,412	14,513
Percentage Owning a ...				
Motorcycle		15%	13%	11%
Boat		15%	14%	15%
Travel Trailer		10%	8%	8%
ATV/ATC			4%	4%
Powered Golf Cart			1%	1%
Number Responding		7,276	16,433	15,157
Percentage Actively Involved in Any Community Group				44%
Number Responding				15,233
Percentage Regularly Engaging in Activity Requiring Active Participation				
38%				
Number Responding				15,199

Courtesy Foremost Insurance Co.

MARKET DATA USERS' SERVICE
NATIONWIDE REPORT
(cont.)

III. MOBILE HOME INFORMATION

	1981	1984	1987	1990
Mobile Home Model Year				
Before 1977	77%	64%	54%	46%
1977-1981	23%	27%	23%	21%
1982-1986	0%	9%	21%	22%
1987-1991	0%	0%	2%	10%
Total Percentage	100%	100%	100%	99%
Number Responding	6,767	7,148	15,933	14,873
Median Model Year	1973	1974	1976	1978
Percentage Owning a Multi-Section MH	20%	22%	20%	25%
Number Responding	6,680	7,178	16,121	14,903
Exterior Siding				
Aluminum	94%	89%	84%	76%
Masonite	4%	6%	7%	9%
Wood	2%	4%	6%	8%
Vinyl				8%
Other	0%	1%	3%	0%
Total Percentage	100%	100%	100%	101%
Number Responding	6,908	7,205	16,202	15,069
Percentage Tied Down				51%
Number Responding				15,024
Acreage				
Located in a MH Park				44%
Less than 1 Acre				21%
1-4 Acres				20%
5-24 Acres				10%
25 Acres or More				5%
Total Percentage				10%
Number Responding				15,159
Items Their MH Has				
Satellite Dish			6%	7%
Skirting			75%	83%
Garage/Shed			64%	59%
Air Conditioning			70%	74%
Electricity				99%
Smoke Detector				89%
Deadbolt Locks on Exterior Doors				31%
Earthquake Stabilizing Device				3%
Fire Alarm to Fire/Central Station				2%
Burglar Alarm to Police/Central Station				1%
None of These				0%
Number Responding*			16,420	15,344

*The percentage totals over 100% due to multiple responses.

Courtesy Foremost Insurance Co.

MARKET DATA USERS' SERVICE
NATIONWIDE REPORT
(cont.)

	1981	1984	1987	1990
Approximate Value of Unattached Structures such as a Shed/Garage/Satellite Dish/Barn				
None			31%	29%
Less than $500			23%	18%
$500-$1,999			23%	23%
$2,000-$4,999			13%	14%
$5,000 and Over			11%	16%
Total Percentage			101%	100%
Number Responding			14,773	13,751
Mobile Home Location				
Park—Don't Own Land	43%	44%	40%	37%
Park/Subdivision—Own Land	5%	6%	5%	6%
Condominium/Co-Op Park	0%	1%	1%	1%
Owner's Private Property	33%	34%	36%	39%
Someone Else's Property	19%	15%	18%	17%
Total Percentage	100%	100%	100%	100%
Number Responding	6,943	7,256	16,464	15,331
Current Monthly Park Rent				
Less than $100	62%	39%	41%	20%
$100-$149	28%	32%	30%	24%
$150-$199	8%	19%	22%	24%
$200 and Over	2%	10%	17%	31%
Total Percentage	100%	100%	100%	99%
Number Responding	2,938	3,156	6,208	5,279
Median Park Rent	$86	$111	$130	$159
Monthly Park Rent One Year Ago				
Less than $100				23%
$100-$149				26%
$150-$199				25%
$200 and Over				26%
Total Percentage				100%
Number Responding				5,008
Median Park Rent One Year Ago				$150
Monthly Park Rent Two Years Ago				
Less than $100				27%
$100-$149				27%
$150-$199				25%
$200 and Over				21%
Total Percentage				100%
Number Responding				4,633
Median Park Rent Two Years Ago				$140
Number of Spaces in MH Park/Subdivision/Condo/Co-Op MH Park				
Less than 50 Spaces		22%	36%	22%
50-99 Spaces		16%	18%	17%
100-199 Spaces		22%	22%	22%
200-299 Spaces		16%	14%	14%
300 Spaces or More		24%	21%	25%
Total Percentage		100%	101%	100%
Number Responding		3,468	7,313	6,451

Courtesy Foremost Insurance Co.

MARKET DATA USERS' SERVICE
NATIONWIDE REPORT
(cont.)

IV. PURCHASE AND FINANCE INFORMATION

	1981	**1984**	**1987**	**1990**
Year MH Was Purchased				
Before 1977	51%	35%	24%	19%
1977-1981	49%	45%	28%	22%
1982-1986	0%	19%	45%	35%
1987-1990	0%	0%	3%	24%
Total Percentage	100%	99%	100%	100%
Number Responding	6,614	7,192	16,347	14,633
Median Year MH Purchased	1976	1978	1981	1983
Mobile Home Purchase Source				
New from Dealer	48%	43%	44%	44%
New from MH Park	5%	5%	3%	3%
New from MH Broker		4%	2%	1%
Used from Dealer	7%	7%	8%	10%
Used from Private Party	34%	33%	34%	33%
Used from MH Park	2%	2%	2%	2%
Used from Real Estate Agent	2%	3%	4%	5%
Used from MH Broker	2%	2%	2%	2%
Total Percentage	100%	99%	99%	100%
Number Responding	6,640	7,162	15,601	14,737
Purchase Price				
Less than $5,000	17%	14%	14%	10%
$5,000-$9,999	37%	31%	26%	20%
$10,000-$14,999	21%	21%	20%	19%
$15,000-$19,999	12%	15%	17%	17%
$20,000-$29,999	9%	13%	15%	19%
$30,000-$39,999	6%	6%	6%	7%
$40,000 and Over	1%	2%	3%	6%
Total Percentage	100%	100%	100%	100%
Number Responding	5,702	6,440	14,962	13,699
Median Purchase Price	$9,000	$10,500	$12,000	$15,000
Market Value				
Less than $5,000	20%	17%	20%	18%
$5,000-$9,999	30%	27%	26%	23%
$10,000-$14,999	16%	18%	18%	17%
$15,000-$19,999	12%	13%	12%	12%
$20,000-$29,999	12%	13%	12%	13%
$30,000-$39,999	6%	6%	6%	7%
$40,000 and Over	4%	5%	5%	10%
Total Percentage	100%	99%	99%	100%
Number Responding	6,228	5,768	14,427	13,129
Median Market Value	$9,900	$10,000	$10,000	$11,000
Percentage Currently Financing MH	42%	42%	42%	39%
Number Responding	6,914	7,169	15,951	14,969
Percentage Financing at Time of MH Purchase	67%	64%	65%	67%
Number Responding	6,693	7,230	15,710	14,703

Courtesy Foremost Insurance Co.

3
Manufactured Home Construction

If your memory goes back several decades, you may think of manufactured homes as being 8 feet wide, perhaps 30 feet long, with a flat roof, aluminum cladding on the exterior, and an interior of cheap plywood paneling. If that is how you visualize manufactured homes, you will find all that has changed, and manufactured homes now have a new look.

In 1980, the United States Congress adopted the name "manufactured home" to replace the name "mobile home." The homes had evolved so that the factory-built home was no longer "mobile," except for the fact that it was built entirely in a factory, mounted on a steel frame and axle, and towed to its site. Once located on a site, the home was rarely moved again; after being placed on a site, only 5 percent of manufactured homes are ever moved a second time.

THE NEW BUILDING CODE

In its early history, the mobile home was often cheaply made, poorly insulated, and even unsafe, because there was no uniform building code to govern its construction. Today, manufactured homes are built to comply with a building code developed by the Department of Housing and Urban Development, or HUD. The code is called the National Manufactured Home Construction and Safety Standards. Every home has a red and silver seal inside the home, certifying that the home was inspected and complies with the code.

The building code covers such things as structural strength, electrical, plumbing and heating guidelines, energy efficiency, and fire safety.

ROOFS AND SIDING

Manufactured home roofs are no longer flat: most roofs are gable type, sheathed with asphalt shingles and trussed. Some roof trusses (in Schult homes, for example) are scissor trusses, meaning the interior ceilings are cathedral-style. Windows may be bay style; wood or vinyl windows are favored over aluminum windows because of their more weatherproof attributes.

Siding choices may be metal, hardboard, vinyl, or wood, in a variety of colors. In 1990, 74 percent of manufactured homes had aluminum siding; Masonite® (hardboard) siding was the choice on 10 percent of homes; wood and vinyl each accounted for 8 percent of home exteriors. With the addition of a garage or carport, plus proper landscaping, manufactured houses look like any site-built model from curbside.

THE INTERIOR

Inside the manufactured home, you will find that plywood paneling has given way to wallboard ceilings and walls, to eliminate the panelized appearance. By survey, 97.3 percent of respondents used wallboard; only 2.7 percent had UF (urea formaldehyde) hardwood panel walls. For cabinet fronts, 65.8 percent used medium-density UF fiberboard; bathroom vanities had 73.8 percent medium-den-

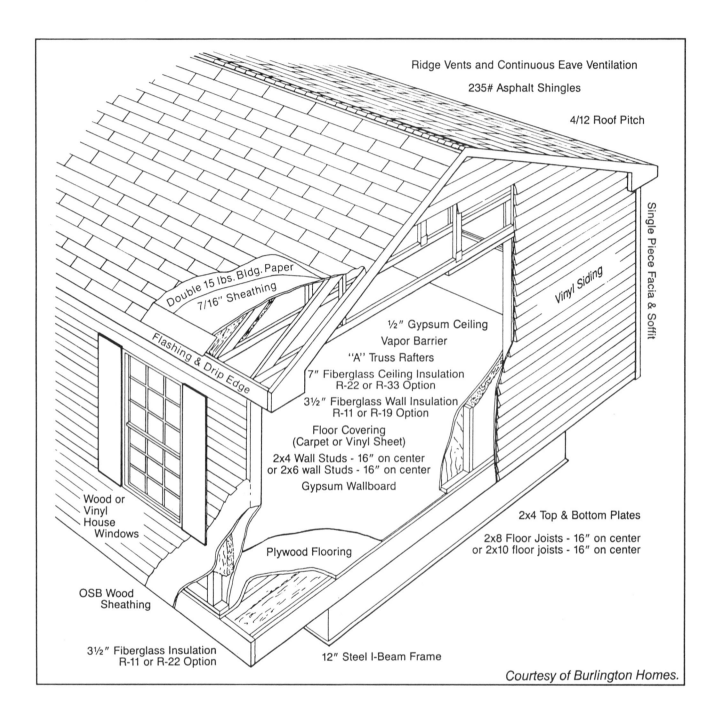

Ridge Vents and Continuous Eave Ventilation

235# Asphalt Shingles

4/12 Roof Pitch

Single Piece Facia & Soffit

Vinyl Siding

Double 15 lbs. Bldg. Paper

7/16" Sheathing

Flashing & Drip Edge

½" Gypsum Ceiling

Vapor Barrier

"A" Truss Rafters

7" Fiberglass Ceiling Insulation
R-22 or R-33 Option

3½" Fiberglass Wall Insulation
R-11 or R-19 Option

Floor Covering
(Carpet or Vinyl Sheet)

2x4 Wall Studs - 16" on center
or 2x6 wall Studs - 16" on center

Gypsum Wallboard

Wood or
Vinyl
House
Windows

Plywood Flooring

2x4 Top & Bottom Plates

2x8 Floor Joists - 16" on center
or 2x10 floor joists - 16" on center

OSB Wood
Sheathing

3½" Fiberglass Insulation
R-11 or R-22 Option

12" Steel I-Beam Frame

Courtesy of Burlington Homes.

sity UF fiberboard fronts. Bathrooms with vanity cabinets and sinks and 54-inch bathtubs with shower heads make the baths more roomy than the cramped baths common in older manufactured homes.

APPLIANCES AND SYSTEMS

Scaled down appliances, once common in manufactured homes, have also been abandoned. Today the appliance package may include a 30-inch free-standing cooking range and a power exhaust range hood with light. A 15 cubic foot, two-door refrigerator/freezer can easily store food to feed a small family for several weeks. A 30-gallon electric water heater ensures that you will not run out of hot water (larger water heaters are an option), and a gas furnace can be adapted to burn either natural or propane gas. Even in the single-wide 14 footer, there is a utility room to hold both washer and dryer. The unit is fitted with copper wiring and a 100-amp electrical service, enough to power all your appliances, with 200-amp service an option.

STRENGTH AND DURABILITY TO MATCH SITE-BUILT HOMES

Perhaps the most important advance in manufactured home construction building codes is the increased strength and durability gained by adopting standards equal to those of the site-built home. For example, a single-wide (14-foot) manufactured home (specifications for a Schult home; others may vary) has a basement-type steel I-beam frame underneath, supporting 2 x 6 floor joists framed on 16-inch centers (16 O.C.) The sidewall studs are 2 x 4s framed on 16-inch centers; 2 x 4s framed on wider 24-inch centers are commonly used on site-built homes, and indeed are approved by national and local building codes. The roof is framed with truss-type rafters set 24 inches O.C. and sheathed with foam core board over the trusses.

When fitted with 3 ½-inch batts of fiberglass insulation, this construction results in R-11 insulation in the walls, R-11 insulation in the floors, and R-11 (blown fiberglass insulation) in the ceilings. The prospective buyer should check to see if these insulation standards meet local R-value requirements.

ENERGY EFFICIENCY

If you refer to Chapter 2, Who Buys Manufactured Homes?, you will see that one of the most common complaints against manufactured homes — by 25 percent of survey respondents — was that the homes were difficult and expensive to heat/cool because of poor insulation. Manufactured home dealers may provide a heavier insulation package than the sample we have mentioned above. Where higher R-values are demanded, the manufactured home dealer will offer a more efficient insulation package. That is the reason, if you are shopping for a pre-owned manufactured home, you should check the insulation package to be sure the home was built to meet your particular local standards. For example, do not buy a home that was built to meet lower southern insulation standards, and then tow it north where the construction would not meet higher energy efficiency standards. The National Manufactured Home Construction and Safety Standards mandate that homes be built with energy efficiency levels to meet the three different temperature zones of the United States. Check the *heating certificate*, which specifies the temperature zone for which the home is designed, and the *comfort cooling certificate*, which specifies size and type of central air conditioner to be used in the home. Both certificates can be found posted inside the home, and you should be sure you are placing your home in the climate area for which it was designed.

Optional Energy Packages

Most manufactured homes are offered with optional energy packages for more severe (cold) climates, but keep in mind that having lower R-values for warmer climates may actually be a mistake. It may make sense to opt for lower insulation standards for a home that will be sited in San Diego, California, or in Honolulu, Hawaii, where temperatures are ideal, and it gets neither very hot nor very cold. But in parts of the south, where winters are moderate but summer temperatures can be brutally hot, a home should have the best energy efficiency possible. The point is that thermal or energy efficiency needs are dictated by the cost of conditioning (heating/cooling) air, and energy costs for air conditioning in hot climates are just as onerous as energy costs for winter heating in the frigid northern states.

Our advice then is always to be concerned with energy efficiency, and to invest in any optional energy upgrades that are offered by the manufacturer. For example, Schult homes offers an optional program called Energy Guard that includes 2 x 6 sidewall framing with R-19 insulation; R-25 blown ceiling insulation; R-11 fiberglass floor insulation; and house-type front and rear exterior doors with storm windows.

The Importance of Energy Efficiency

The need for all the energy efficiency you can possibly buy is demonstrated in an Associated Press article (*Minneapolis Star Tribune*, February 3, 1992) datelined Clemson, SC. The article quoted Lawrence P. Golan, director of the South Carolina Energy Research and Development Center at Clemson University, as noting that "some of the power bills are enormous" for manufactured housing. The residential energy costs for the state (all homes) are more than $1 billion annually, and the efficiency of manufactured homes is under scrutiny because these homes make up more than 40 percent of South Carolina's new home sales.

Because energy bills can be a major factor in manufactured home budgets, you should shop carefully for a home that is energy efficient. Jack Ireton-Hewitt, president of Burlington Homes of New England, Inc., says that for homes in the Maine-New England area, Burlington has chosen to install only all-vinyl Thermopane windows.

Check Energy Efficiency Ratings on Appliances

Check the efficiency not only of the structure itself, but the EER (energy efficiency rating) of each of the major appliances and of the furnace itself. The higher the EER, the more efficient the appliance. A

forced air gas furnace should have an efficiency rating of 90 or more: several manufacturers, such as Lennox, make furnaces that are 97 percent efficient. Remember, too, that lifestyle plays a major role in energy bills, and energy costs vary widely between homes of the exact same style.

THE IMPORTANCE OF THE SITE TO ENERGY EFFICIENCY

If energy bills are very high for manufactured homes, one major factor may be found in the choice of a site for the home. In the early days, mobile home parks were laid out on a flat pasture or former corn or wheat field, with no shade or windbreaks to aid in sheltering the home. If you will be buying your own home site, shop for a site that has many mature trees to provide cooling and shade in summer and to serve as windbreaks in winter. If necessary, plant several rows of pines or other evergreen trees as a windbreak against prevailing winter blasts.

CONSIDER HEAT LOSS THROUGH THE FLOOR

Another potential energy loser is lack of a foundation or skirting around the base of the manufactured home. Because we all know that hot air rises, it is a common mistake to underestimate the heat loss downward, or through the floor. But heat loss can go in any direction. In fact, for the site-built home with average insulation, weatherstripping, and storm windows, the greatest heat loss occurs through the basement walls. Heat will flow to cold, and it will flow *downward* if that is the path of least resistance for heat transfer. Manufactured home floors should be fitted with a maximum of insulation, with floor R-values of 19 or more the goal. (Six inches of fiberglass batt will provide R-19.) A good quality pad and carpeting also can add more R-value to floors than tile or vinyl floor covering, so in cold climates you may opt for all-carpeted floors. Also, regardless of the amount of floor insulation, it is best to install skirting that is not only attractive but that provides insulation value at the base around the home's perimeter.

Exploded view shows construction of manufactured homes. Building codes parallel the code requirements for stick-built homes. Factory technology and controlled climate permit construction economies and lower cost of housing. Courtesy of the Manufactured Housing Institute.

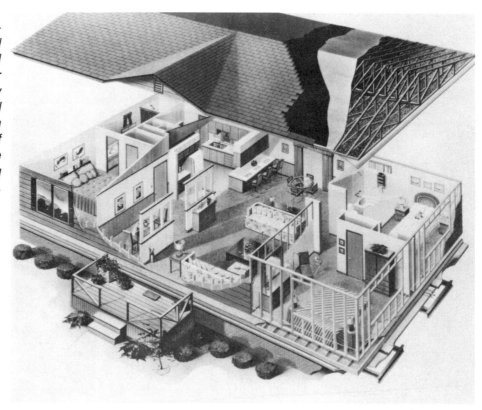

Huge factory floor area permits construction to proceed on many homes simultaneously. Home floors are assembled on the steel frames, which enable the homes to be towed to their sites. Courtesy of the Manufactured Housing Institute.

Building components, such as kitchen cabinets and interior partitions, can be positioned along the home assembly line, for easy retrieval by workers. Courtesy of the Manufactured Housing Institute.

Entire wall panels can be assembled flat on platforms, tipped into place on home floor. This type of assembly eliminates the wasted effort of climbing scaffolding. Courtesy of the Manufactured Housing Institute.

Foam insulation board installed over fiberglass batts in stud cavities ensures high energy efficiency. Note steel inlet wall bracing in front of worker at left of photo. Courtesy of the Manufactured Housing Institute.

Component assembly area holds racks of pre-hung doors, paneling, and insulation board, along with workbenches for on-site assembly. Courtesy of the Manufactured Housing Institute.

Superior organization of factory construction is demonstrated in this photo. On the floor deck workers install partitions, while a third worker installs the electrical wiring on an outside wall partition. Courtesy of the Manufactured Housing Institute.

The entire ceiling/roof can be assembled at one work station, raised and nailed into place atop the walls of the home. Courtesy of the Manufactured Housing Institute.

Roof trusses are installed on this low-slope roof assembly, and will be raised into place atop the home in one piece. Courtesy of the Manufactured Housing Institute.

Full-length scaffolding permits workers to install roof insulation batts with minimum labor. Courtesy of the Manufactured Housing Institute.

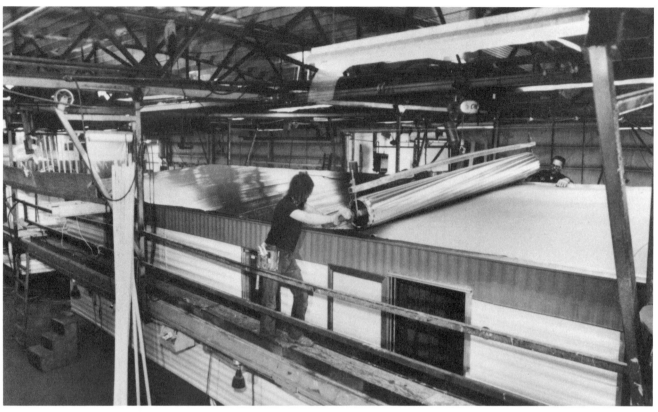

Two workers unroll metal (aluminum) roof sheeting on the roof of a single-wide home.
Courtesy of the Manufactured Housing Institute.

One worker uses an airgun to staple asphalt shingles on the roof, while another installs siding using a power nailer. Courtesy of the Manufactured Housing Institute.

When set up on a site with landscaping and a closed foundation, even modest manufactured homes can provide attractive and low-cost housing. Courtesy of the Manufactured Housing Institute.

4
Choosing a Home Site

The Manufactured Housing Institute recommends that before you choose a home, you should choose a site for the home. If you choose the home first, and then go in search of a home site, you may find that for one or more reasons you cannot place your new manufactured home on the site of your choice. As we will discuss, there are many roadblocks that might be encountered to placing your new home. Consider our list carefully to make the buying experience as pleasant as possible and to avoid not only possible financial loss but also wasted time.

OPTIONS FOR SITE SELECTION

The Pre-Owned Home

There are several options for site selection. First, you may opt to buy a pre-owned manufactured home that is already located in a community park or on private land. This way, you will know that all utilities are available and all questions of code restrictions have already been settled. Buyers of pre-owned manufactured homes buy their homes from private owners (33 percent), from dealers (10 percent), or from real estate agents (5 percent.) Buying a pre-owned manufactured home means you will avoid all problems of placement, such as restrictions or utility availability.

Siting on Your Own Land

A second option is planning to set up your new manufactured home on land you own or intend to buy. Of all buyers of new manufactured homes, 39 percent place their homes on their own private property, and another 6 percent locate their homes on lots bought in a park or a subdivision.

Siting on Rented Land

The third option is to locate the home on rented land, or on a home site on which you pay rent, in a park or manufactured home community. Of new buyers, 37 percent locate their homes on a lot in a park; 17 percent of home buyers locate their homes on private property that is not a home park.

If you are not sure whether you want to buy a home site or simply to rent a site in a park or on private land, start by checking lot rental prices in your area. Rental rates are rising, and increasing park rents are one of the sources of dissatisfaction of living in a manufactured home, as listed by 26 percent of survey respondents. The current median park rent (latest available figures are for 1990) is $159.00 per month, up from a median park rent of $140.00 in 1988, just two years previous. This represents an annual increase in rent of nearly 7 percent per year. Of park rentals, the survey shows that 23 percent rent for less than $100; 26 percent rent for $100-$149; 25 percent rent for $150-$199, and 26 percent for $200 or more. These rental figures should help you make a decision on whether renting or owning a site best fits your monthly housing budget.

The Manufactured Housing Institute (MHI) suggests that you consider carefully where you will locate your new home. The following guidelines from the MHI should help you avoid any error in choice and help you anticipate the sorts of problems you may encounter with each of the three site choices.

A PLACE OF YOUR OWN

You may plan on the privacy and independence of

When sited in planned home communities, with well-landscaped lawns, the manufactured homes can provide affordable housing. Courtesy of the Manufactured Housing Institute.

Gently rolling terrain and mature trees can enhance the curb appeal of individual homes while helping to reduce energy costs. Courtesy of the Manufactured Housing Institute.

Curving lot lines and cul de sac siting can add to development appeal for manufactured home sites. Wooded area beyond can become a nature area, with walks and bikeways for recreation. Courtesy of the Manufactured Housing Institute.

having your own manufactured home placed on your own lot or acreage. But before you purchase that piece of land, or make final plans, check with local building officials to learn of any restrictions that might complicate that placement, or even prevent you from carrying out your plan at all.

The first step is to check out any zoning requirements or restrictions that you will encounter. In many areas, there are prohibitions against manufactured homes, or restrictions regarding the size and exterior appearance of homes that may be located within city, suburb, or county boundaries. Check the phone book for the telephone number of the community's Building Department or Land Use Department, and ask local officials for advice and direction on what restrictions may apply.

Restrictive Covenants

Restrictive covenants are limitations listed on property deeds that dictate or control how the land parcel may be used. Some of these restrictions may not in fact be constitutional, and the MHI and HUD are working to remove illegal restrictions. (There has been little to stop local politicos from passing discriminatory covenants. The only recourse has been for the individual to engage in legal conflict with the local governing body, a lengthy and expensive process. It is not true that you cannot fight city hall: you just cannot *beat* city hall.) Examples of these restrictive covenants may be those that dictate the size or construction of a dwelling. A title search at the time of purchase may reveal such restrictive covenants, but some of these covenants are written in "legalese" and may be difficult to understand. The best procedure may be to have an experienced real estate attorney conduct the title search for you. Be sure the title search is especially attuned to restrictions that would prohibit you from locating a manufactured home on the site.

Availability of Utilities

Manufactured homes are fully plumbed and wired when you buy them, but you must hook up the home to electrical, water, and sewerage facilities. If you are locating the home in an established park community, such facilities are already in place. If you are placing the home on your own property, you must check to be sure that all the utilities are available.

If your land is within an incorporated city, the question of access to utilities is probably a given; but if you intend to place the home on your own rural property, you may find utilities either unavailable or very expensive to obtain.

Electrical power. If the site for your home is in a remote rural or recreational area, be very sure that there are electrical power lines nearby. If there are no electrical power lines close by, the usual procedure is for the customer to pay to extend the line from the nearest source to the site. If that power line extension is to be made over a long distance, getting access to electrical power can easily become a problem costing thousands of dollars. Check with your local power company to find out where the power line is and how much it would cost to extend electrical service to your property.

Water supplies. Water and sewer service will be available in the streets if your proposed site is within incorporated city limits. But if your site is rural or remote, you may have to find your own water source; i.e., drill your own well.

In some areas, there are plentiful underground water sources, so you can drill a well at almost any point and find water. In areas where underground water is in good supply, the only question may be how deep you must drill to find a water source. (The cost of drilling a well is usually figured on both the size of the pipe you must use, dictated by building or plumbing codes, and the depth you must drill. So the formula, depending on the area where you live and local drilling costs, will be X-dollars/inch pipe diameter/per foot of depth.) Ranchers and farmers in arid areas can sometimes pay for drilling deep wells because they will be using the water for business purposes, but drilling a deep well can become prohibitively expensive if you are drilling to serve a single household.

In many areas, either there may be no underground water veins at all, or water at that location may be of very poor quality — it may either be excessively hard water or have a high iron content. Either the minerals in hard water or high iron content can stain and damage plumbing fixtures and can make the water quite unpalatable.

Before investing in a site, check with local well-drilling contractors to learn whether water is accessible at your site, and at what cost. Check with both the well driller and local health authorities to be sure that there will be no water quality problems with water from your well. Do not forget to add the cost of a well to the site cost.

Sewerage. You must also have accessible to your site a sewer system for waste disposal. As in the case of water and electrical supplies, home sites within city limits will usually have municipal sewer facilities available. If city sewer is not available, you must build your own sewer system, installing a septic tank and drain field. Building your own septic system can be an acceptable solution to lack of municipal sewerage facilities at your site, but depending on several factors, it can also be expensive and add substantially to the total cost of your home site.

To learn the codes governing septic system construction for your area, check with your local building and/or plumbing inspector. (Smaller localities may have an inspector for all areas of the building codes. Larger communities may have specialized inspectors.) The size and cost of your septic system will be dictated by the local code and will also be affected by the number of people who will share the home and use the sewer facilities.

Before approving your permit for a septic system, the building department will ask for a sample of the soil at your site, or a percolation test. The term *percolation* refers to the rate at which the soil in your site can absorb waste water from the septic system. If soil is light and sandy, or if there is a gravel base beneath the surface of your site that can readily absorb waste water, the septic system will not need an extensive leach (drain) field for waste water dispersal. But if the soil does not have a good percolation rate — i.e., cannot readily absorb waste

water — you may have to install an extensive and expensive leach field. Heavy clay soil, for example, will often have a very poor water absorption rate, or percolation rate, and is therefore not suitable for use of a septic system.

If soil tests reveal poor percolation rates at your site, the septic or plumbing contractor can excavate long (and wide) trenches, extend water drain pipes through the trenches, and then fill the trenches with a gravel base. This will solve the percolation problem because the waste water then will obviously disperse easily through the loose gravel fill. However, because of the extensive excavation and the cost of gravel and extra drain pipes, it is a very expensive solution that can add substantially to your site costs.

As one can see, there may be many pitfalls to buying a site and setting up a manufactured home. The pitfalls are by no means insurmountable, but you should be aware of the possible problems and be prepared, both in time and financial resources, to overcome any unforeseen problems.

RENTING A SITE IN A PLANNED COMMUNITY

Another option for placing your home is to rent or lease a site in a community developed especially for manufactured homes. While many people prefer to have the privacy and freedom of living on their own property, the option of renting a developed site obviously can be a less complicated choice, because all the code and zoning approvals and the utilities necessary are already in place. If you do not have the time or money to invest in and develop your own site, this may be a more suitable option for you.

Before you decide to locate your manufactured home in a planned community, consider the following list of consumer precautions, as recommended by the Manufactured Housing Institute:

❑ Visit communities in the area where you would like to live. Some manufactured home dealers may operate their own rental facilities, so do not neglect to query the dealer about his own — or other — rental communities.

❏ Check out what amenities each community offers, such as garages or carports, wading or swimming pools, tennis courts, play areas, and other recreational amenities.

❏ Check rental costs, installation costs, and any miscellaneous service charges: who shovels the snow and mows the lawn, and who pays for the services? Is garbage/trash pickup extra, or is it included in the site rent?

❏ Is a written lease required, and how long is the lease?

❏ What are charges for utility connections and other services?

❏ Who installs the home on the site, the dealer or you, the owner?

❏ What are the charges for installing the home?

❏ What about street maintenance and mail?

❏ What are the community rules and bylaws? Can you have pets, or install a storage shed?

❏ Are there community restrictions covering resale of your home?

❏ What happens if the owner of the park community sells the property for other purposes, and you must move the home because of the sale? Will the owner aid you in any way to find or move to another park or location?

BUYING A HOME AND SITE IN A PLANNED COMMUNITY

The last alternative is to buy a manufactured home, complete and placed on its site in a planned community. Just as renting a site in a planned community is less complicated than setting up a home on your own property, so, too, are there fewer problems when you buy an established home in a planned community because you do not have to worry about placement. Still, a few precautions are in order.

Check into the Community Before Buying

The MHI advises you to check into the costs, services, and rules of any community before buying to be sure you will be happy living there. Keep in mind that the survey quoted in Chapter 2 on disadvantages of living in a manufactured home showed that 21 percent of respondents complained about poor maintenance, unacceptable rules and restrictions, and personal conflicts with the owner/manager of the park. Add in another 8 percent who worried that their park would be sold for other purposes, forcing them to move, and you have a high ratio of dissatisfaction related directly to drawbacks that might be avoided if only buyers would be more careful in the site selection process.

The MHI also urges that you consider the points covered in the previous section, Renting a Site in a Planned Community. Many or most of the tips that apply to a rented site also would apply to buying that site in a planned community.

Site Energy Awareness

As mentioned in Chapter 2, a survey of owners showed that a major source of dissatisfaction with manufactured home living was high energy bills for heating and cooling the space. The survey showed that fully 25 percent of home owners were unhappy with heating and cooling costs.

In the past, these complaints were often caused by poor insulation or other construction, or by inefficient appliances, including the heating and cooling equipment. The manufacturers of the homes have addressed the problems of thermal efficiency by adopting strict building codes that govern construction and insulation standards. But home siting, too, was and is part of the problem of high energy consumption.

We should recognize that an important factor contributing to high energy consumption is that many manufactured homes are placed on bare lots or in parks that were developed in former flatlands such as corn fields. These flat sites are obviously easy and inexpensive to develop, and require little earth movement or excavation. There are no trees to bulldoze or to grade around.

The Importance of Landscaping

But research has shown that a major factor in reducing energy costs for the manufactured (or any) home is the landscaping, including the way the land itself is contoured, plus the presence of trees to offer summer shade and winter windbreaks.

You should survey any potential site, whether your own private land or a rented or purchased park site, to see whether the landscaping helps shelter the home. Keep in mind that the presence of other manufactured homes helps to buffer the wind from striking your home. Tests have shown that air moving over exterior walls — whether it is hot or cold air — accelerates the transfer of heat-to-cold movement through those walls. So wind or air movement over the exterior of your home will increase heat loss or gain through those walls and will raise energy costs.

There is little you can do if lack of land contours and lack of trees are problems on developed park sites. But you can seek out parks or communities that feature mature trees and other landscaping to shelter your home, and avoid those flatland parks with no protective landscaping.

On Your Own Site

If you are buying your own home site, you can, of course, do a number of things that will help control energy costs. You could hire an excavating contractor to throw up an earth berm as a windbreak, or you might plant several rows of dense evergreen trees to serve as a windrow or windbreak along the side of your site from which the prevailing winter winds blow.

Other options might be to build a garage on the cold — usually the north — side of the home. Also, in most home park communities, you must install skirting to cover the space between the bottom edge of the home and the ground. The parks may require skirting for aesthetic purposes, to improve the curb appeal of your home and the appearance of the park generally. And even decorative skirting can stop the wind from blowing underneath the home and contributing to heat loss through the floor. But you should install a foundation or skirting that has insulating value, because much of your heat loss will otherwise be through the floor.

Remember, too, that any shrubs planted around the foundation perimeter can also help to buffer the wind and to conserve energy, while improving the looks and curb appeal of your site.

Minor amenities, such as the plant window, shutters, and gabled porch roof, can help soften the "boxy" appearance of single-wide homes. Courtesy of the Manufactured Housing Institute.

Paved drives, landscaping, and wooded siting provide good background effect for manufactured homes. Courtesy of the Manufactured Housing Institute.

A front bow window, paved walk and drive, faux stone foundation enclosure, and deck-sized roofed porch are low-cost additions that enhance the curb appeal of this home. Courtesy of the Manufactured Housing Institute.

5
Choosing a Manufactured Home

You can buy a manufactured home from a real estate agent (if the home is already placed in a park community); direct from a home manufacturing company, via their own retail sales offices; or from a retail home sales center that may sell homes built by several different manufacturers. Surveys reveal that 44 percent of respondents bought their manufactured home new, from a dealer; 33 percent bought their home used from a private party; 10 percent bought the home used from a dealer; 5 percent bought used manufactured homes through real estate agents; and small percentages bought their homes from various other sources. Two-thirds, or 67 percent, financed their manufactured home purchase.

FINDING A HOME DEALER

Choose your home dealer carefully. The dealer will help you choose your home and suitable options and may have to custom-order the home from the factory. Be aware, too, that delivery and proper installation are very important, and your dealer should either take care of these important steps for you or should arrange with subcontractors who will handle transportation and installation. The dealer will arrange home financing and insurance if necessary, and he will also be the one you contact far into the future if any warranty service is needed. Because the dealer can become an important person in your life for a period covering many years, the Manufactured Housing Institute (MHI) urges that you use

the same care in selecting a dealer as you use in selecting the home itself.

Locating a Reputable Dealer

How can you be sure you have found a reputable home dealer? If you have friends or relatives who live in manufactured homes, ask them for dealer referrals, and also ask them to suggest a respected home manufacturer. Also, check in the Appendix of this book for the phone number or address of your state manufactured home association, and ask the association for a list of dealers and manufacturers in your area. When you have narrowed your list down to a couple of dealers, call the Better Business Bureau and ask whether the particular dealer(s) has any customer complaints on file, or if there is any history of unresolved complaints against the dealer or his associates.

As with any major purchase, you should shop several dealers and study the construction, energy efficiency, and warranties of the homes offered by each manufacturer. Following are ideas to keep in mind when shopping the home market, as suggested by the Manufactured Housing Institute in their brochure, "How To Buy a Manufactured Home."

EXTERIOR CHOICES

Siding
If you know where you will locate your home, you may already have an idea of what color and type of

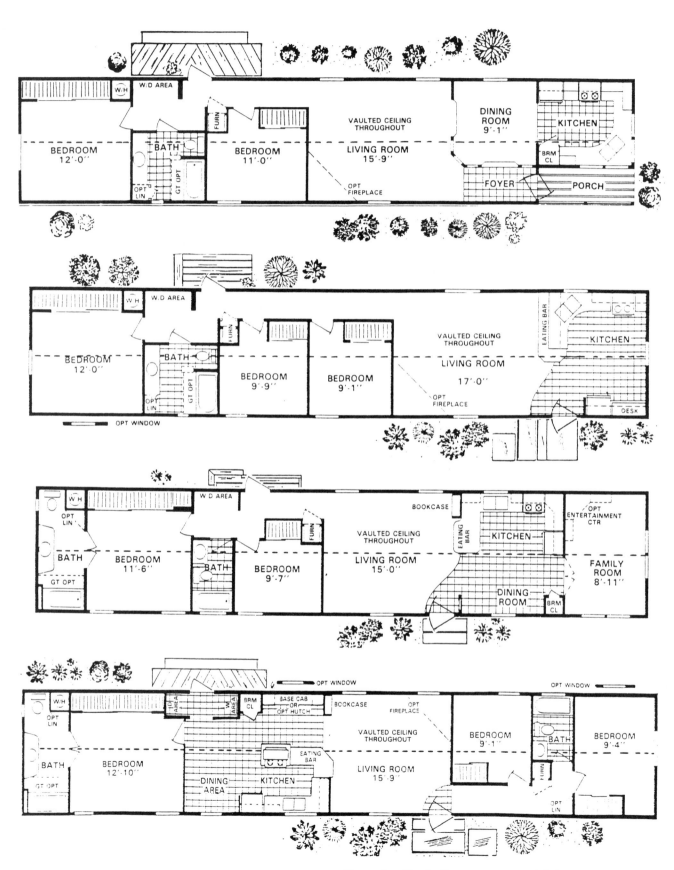

Floor plan illustrations courtesy of Schult Homes Corp.

siding will fit in with houses around you. Exterior siding options include the most popular metal (76 percent of homes have aluminum siding), with hardboard, vinyl, and wood siding each having about 8 percent of the home market. Note that, in the interest of uniformity, some manufactured home communities have restrictions on the style and siding choice of the homes placed on their sites. For example, some suburban and rural park communities we have seen insist that all homes within the community have wood siding, for a rustic and natural look.

Windows, Roofs, and Other Options

Other exterior options available may include bay windows, skylights or roof windows, with windows made from wood, vinyl, or aluminum. Most manufactured homes today have a pitched (sloped) roof with asphalt shingles, and some may have a front gable on the roof. Exterior options include window awnings, patio covers, decks, steps, and skirting or enclosures around the crawlspace.

Sizes and Floor Plans

Size of homes and floor plans available are almost unlimited in variety. Manufactured homes may range in size from 400 square feet of floor space up to 2,500 square feet. Floor plans offer large living rooms, multiple bedrooms, formal dining rooms, fully equipped kitchens with eating bars, two or more bathrooms, and utility rooms for laundry and heating equipment. If your needs are modest, you can opt for a single-wide home; if you have a large enough lot, you may opt for a multi-section design. The most opulent manufactured home we have heard of has an indoor swimming pool and costs upwards of $300,000.00.

Consider Plans to Relocate

Do you have even remote plans to relocate your home at a later date? Before buying a home, check out laws for moving your home through each state involved. Laws vary widely by state, but be aware that some states, especially eastern states, have regulations limiting the size, weight, or width of homes that may be transported on state highways. Note that you must not only check the laws in the state in which you live but also the laws of every state through which you will move the home. And, of course, you will have the expense of moving your home, and license fees for each state through which you will pass, plus costs for foundation construction, installation, and utility hookups at the new living site. All things considered, it may be cheaper to sell a home at its present site and buy a new home at the new location to which you want to move. Or, if you intend to move within only a few years, it may be more prudent to delay purchase of the new manufactured home until you have made your move.

ENERGY OPTIONS

As we have noted elsewhere, the National Manufactured Home Construction and Safety Standards set separate energy efficiency levels for each of three different U.S. temperature zones. You should be aware that energy codes for any new home tend to be minimum requirements only, and that in almost every case you will easily recover any investment in energy efficiency within a short period of time. Remember also that fully 25 percent of owners in the Foremost Insurance survey (Chapter 2) stated that high energy bills were a major source of dissatisfaction with manufactured home living. This should convince us that it is poor economy to settle for a minimum energy package, when one might buy an upgraded energy package for only a couple thousand dollars more.

Because manufactured homes often have no basements, there is a greater possibility of heat loss through the floors, especially in cold climates. Because of the chances of experiencing large energy losses through the floor of the home, added insulation and energy-saving appliances should be the rule, not an option.

Most manufactured home dealers will be able to offer upgraded energy packages. Ask your salesperson to list all the energy-saving options available. Examples of energy-saving components for your home include:

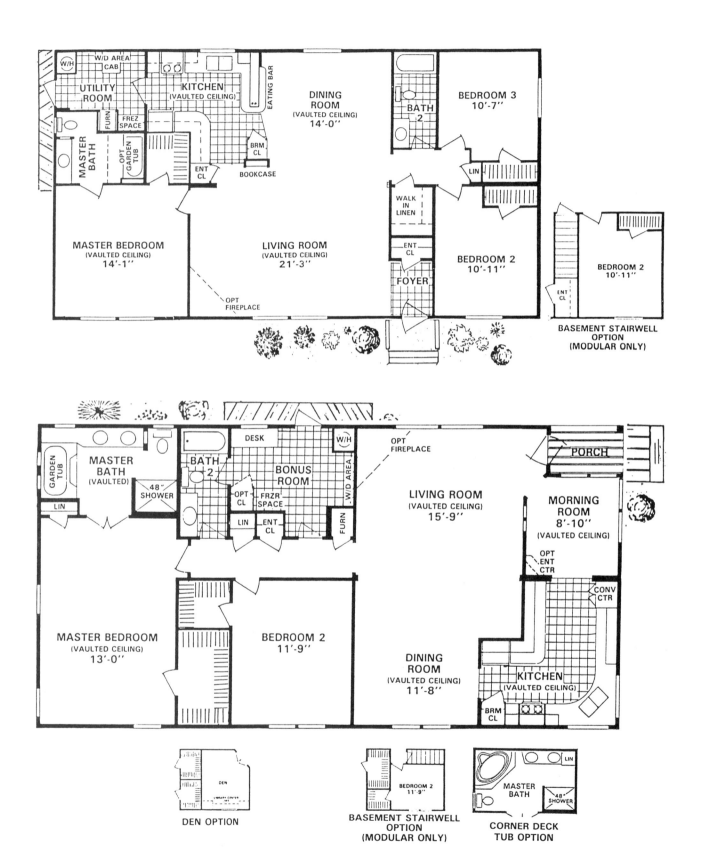

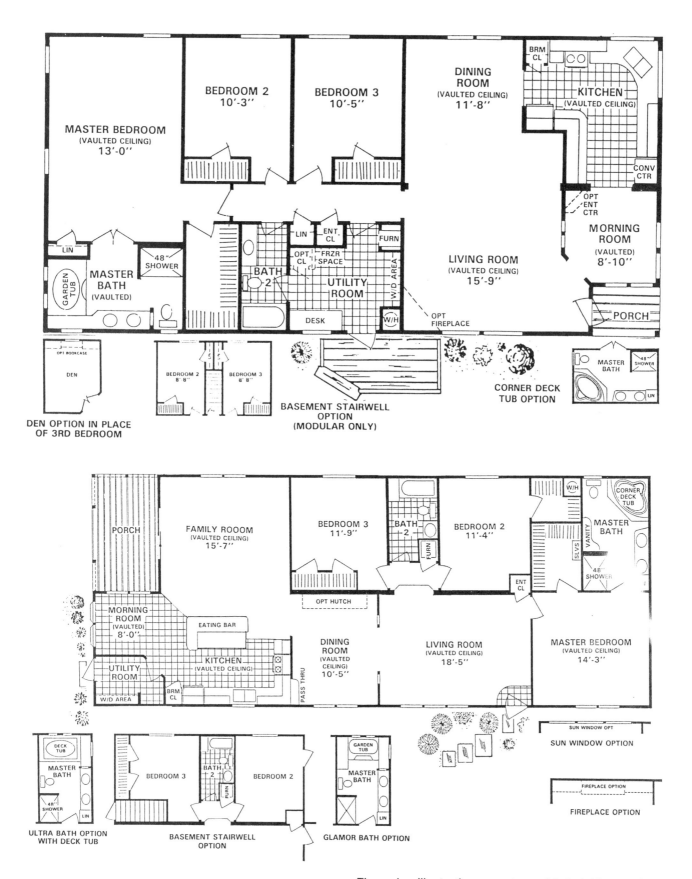

Floor plan illustrations courtesy of Schult Homes Corp.

❏ added insulation
❏ double- or triple-glazed windows
❏ insulating sheathing products
❏ high-efficiency appliances, including water heaters, refrigerators, furnaces, and air conditioners

An important point, too, is that all air distribution ducts, the ducts that distribute heated/cooled air, should be insulated. Metal ducts that are not insulated give off expensive heat by radiation. Energy conservation is enhanced if heated or cooled air is delivered exactly where it is needed, not leaked into unheated wall or ceiling cavities. Again, look for the *heating certificate* that specifies which temperature zone your home was designed for, and also check the *comfort cooling certificate* that lists the proper air conditioning equipment for your home. You can place the highest-rated home in any warmer climate, but do not place a home with a lower energy rating in a colder climate, because you will be certain to be disappointed both with the comfort level and with the energy costs for that misplaced home.

BUILDING SPECIFICATIONS

Ask your dealer to supply you with a list of building specifications for the home(s) you are considering. Are walls 2 x 4 or 2 x 6 construction? Do you have an option of buying the thicker 2 x 6 walls, which are not only stronger but also can hold thicker fiberglass insulation batts? What size are the floor joists? They should be at least 2 x 6s, preferably 2 x 8s. Are floors covered with plywood, oriented strand board, or particle board? What are insulation R-values of walls, ceilings, and floors? Is plumbing piping plastic or copper? Be aware that in very cold climates the unprotected water pipes in manufactured homes (or any home) can freeze. Plastic water pipes cannot be heated to thaw them, and you cannot use electrical heater wraps on plastic pipe. Consider where you are placing the home before making your decision.

What about electrical service? Is it 100 amps or more, as required for handling today's many electrical appliances? Are walls and ceilings finished in wallboard, or in cheaper plywood paneling? Is the factory nearby, and can you arrange a tour to see firsthand how the homes are built?

WARRANTY COVERAGE

The manufactured home structure is usually covered by the manufacturer's warranty. Such items as transportation and installation of the home should also be covered under warranty, but most often these warranties are made by the dealer who sells the home, not by the home's manufacturer. Most dealers and contractors will offer written warranties on transportation and installation of the home. Ask in advance to have copies of any warranties offered, and study these warranties carefully so that you understand just what the warranties cover. Do not wait until there is a problem before knowing your warranty rights.

STANDARD HOME SPECIFICATIONS: HUD CODE

The Department of Housing and Urban Development (HUD) has established standard specifications for manufactured home construction, as listed below. Almost all of the materials specified in the standard HUD code are subject to optional choices, a sample list of which follows the standard list.

Exterior

1. A 4 x 12 pitched roof.
2. 235-lb. asphalt shingles. (Same as stick-built code.)
3. Double application of building paper under shingles.
4. Double 4-inch residential vinyl house siding: exterior walls with wood sheathing.
5. Single-hung vinyl Portland Glass Thermal Pane windows with muntins. Tilting lower sash.
6. 40-lb. test roof rafters. (Same as stick-built code.)
7. Two solid polyurethane-insulated steel doors with adjustable thresholds and Weslock locks.

8. Two combination crossbuck storm doors.

9. Two exterior porch lights.

10. Louvered shutters with *all* windows.

11. Ranch-type exterior profile.

12. Insulation specifications: 3 1/2 inch (R-11) Kraft-faced insulated sidewalls.

13. 2 x 8 floor joists, 16 inches on center.

14. 2 x 4 top and bottom plates.

15. 12-inch I-beam frame.

16. Dormers standard on single-wide.

17. Plywood floor decking.

Interior

1. Miller oil gun furnace, installed in its own enclosure, lined with drywall, complete with air return system.

2. 42-gallon electric water heater with five-year warranty.

3. 100-amp electrical service.

4. 15-cubic foot double-door refrigerator.

5. Free-standing electric range.

6. Custom vinyl-covered Sheetrock® wallboard panels.

7. Cabinet doors and drawer fronts custom-built from native oak.

8. Congoleum® tile with color choice.

9. 2 x 3 interior walls 16 inches on center.

10. Carpet and pad standard in living room and master bedroom, FHA-approved Antron III, 100% nylon.

11. Deluxe sofa/chair/end table/coffee table/lamp — single wides only.

12. Wooden dinette with four chairs — single wides only.

13. Copper water supply lines with shut-offs at all sinks and toilets.

14. Decorative vinyls in all bathrooms.

15. Curtains and drapes color-coordinated with flooring.

16. Bath exhaust fans.

17. 60-inch fiberglass tub with grab bar.

18. Miter joints on all interior door trim.

19. Interior window sills.

20. Stainless steel double-bowl kitchen sink with Delta single lever faucet with spray.

21. Wire and vent for dryer.

22. Exterior receptacle protected by GFCI (Ground Fault Circuit Interrupter).

23. Leviton light switches (paddle fans).

24. Residential molding.

25. Vinyl-coated steel shelving in closets.

26. China lavatory sinks.

27. Delta single lever faucets.

28. One outside water faucet.

29. Six panel passage, closet, and bifold doors.

30. Electric door chimes.

31. Post-formed rolled edge kitchen countertops.

OPTIONS

An almost unlimited number of options are available for the manufactured home. Following is a sample list found in literature obtained from Burlington Homes of New England, Inc. Ask your own dealer to provide you with a full list of available home options.

Appliances

Appliance options include:

• dishwasher

• garbage disposal

• washer and dryer

• trash compactor

• microwave oven

• self-cleaning range

• Jenn-Air range

• 18- or 20-cubic foot refrigerator/freezer, either double-door or side-by-side, or a 20-cubic foot model with ice and water door dispenser, or an icemaker

As with choosing any home, consider curb appeal and resale value carefully before you buy. The multi-section home shown here has all the amenities of a site-built house at significantly lower cost. Courtesy of the Manufactured Housing Institute.

If possible, narrow your home choice down to one or two models, then visit a like model that is already set up. Added amenities, such as the wooden walk, porch/deck, window flower boxes and foundation plantings, can make a marked change in the appearance of the home. Courtesy of the Manufactured Housing Institute.

Windows

Window options include:

- low-E (for low-emissivity) glass with argon gas
- bow and picture windows
- octagon windows
- Walk-a-bay (to the floor) bay windows
- fixed or venting skylights

Doors

Door options include:

- Patio or Atrium-style doors
- side lights at doors
- deadbolt locks
- recessed entry doors

Miscellaneous Exterior Options

In addition to choices of types of siding, exterior options include sectional dormers and a 5/12 roof pitch (on sectional homes).

Insulation

Extra insulation packages would almost without exception be worth buying. The cost of energy is never going to go down, and the cost of energy for manufactured homes (as shown by survey) has been a major complaint for manufactured home owners. Insulation options include an energy efficiency package, extra-thick insulation, and 2 x 6 sidewalls for R-19.

Heat

What sort of heating should you buy for your manufactured home? This manufacturer (Burlington Homes) offers:

- hot water baseboard
- electric baseboard
- a wood-burning fireplace
- perimeter heat registers
- heat pump ready

Electrical

Electrical options to choose from include:

- 200-amp service
- TV jacks built in
- phone jacks
- closet lights
- water heater timer (for energy efficiency)
- separate breaker for heat tape
- air conditioner ready

Plumbing

Options to standard floor plans include:

- half-bath
- $3/4$ bath with a 36-inch shower stall
- tub and shower doors
- handicapped grab rails (by all means: bathtub falls are the most common cause of bathroom accident)
- decorative tub drape
- whirlpool bathtub(s)
- garden tub(s)

Floor Covering

Carpet is often standard, and is a good choice for extra floor insulation. Flooring options include oak wood parquet floors or tile entry.

Wall Covering and Molding

Vinyl-covered drywall (wallboard) panels are standard in these homes. Finished and painted drywall, wainscoting, and chair rail moldings (usually used in kitchen or dining room eating spaces) are wall options.

Cabinets

Triangle Pacific oak cabinets and hutches are optional cabinet choices. Other cabinet choices might include:

- bath cabinet over the toilet
- laundry overhead cabinets
- kitchen convenience center to hold optional stereo or microwave
- pantry
- corner curio cabinets

Kitchen divider cabinet options include corner cabinets, a corner breakfast table, and a dining booth.

Miscellaneous

Other options include paddle (ceiling) fans, an air exchanger, built-in stereo system, cathedral ceilings, attic access (in sectionals), built-in ironing board, and mirrored bifold closet doors.

All the above options are available at extra cost from Burlington Homes of New England, Inc. Most dealers and manufacturers will offer a similar list of options. Be sure you are aware of all your options before making your final buying decision.

NON-DEALER OPTIONS

Companies such as Sears offer a wide array of exterior options for manufactured homes. Sears offers a catalog ("specialog") especially for manufactured home owners. Options include a carport roof and supports for use where no garage is provided. Other options include a selection of storage sheds to provide needed storage space for lawn and sports equipment.

Other useful options include lawn and garden tools, mailboxes (rural type on a post, if no community mail center is provided), and aluminum or canvas awnings. The awnings are a valuable aid for energy conservation and are especially good for homes in communities where there are no trees to provide shade or protection from the wind. Heat gain in summer is especially severe through windows where the sunlight can directly strike the window pane, so use awnings to shade windows on the sunny side of the home.

Other options include steel steps (which also may be available from your dealer). And, if the manufactured home is set on top of piers or concrete blocks so the perimeter around the home base is not closed, install skirting to close the underside of the home against roving animals and blown debris. Skirting can be wood or metal panels purchased from home suppliers.

Interior designs available in manufactured homes can make a home feel spacious and gracious. This interior shot of a double-wide home demonstrates some interior design possibilities. Courtesy of the Manufactured Housing Institute.

Kitchen amenities available include a dishwasher, microwave oven, cooktop exhaust hood, trash compactor, and breakfast bar. Courtesy of the Manufactured Housing Institute.

Spacious interior includes formal dining area with skylight and clerestory window. Ceiling paddle fans aid home cooling, heating. Courtesy of the Manufactured Housing Institute.

Today's manufactured homes have plenty of room for entertaining. Large glass areas bring the outdoors in, make homes seem larger. Courtesy of the Manufactured Housing Institute.

6

Transporting and Installing the Home

When you have made a decision on which manufactured home to buy, you have to plan how you will prepare the site, transport the home to your lot, and accomplish the placement or installation. The steps you will follow include:

- preparing the site
- building the proper foundation
- installing and leveling the home
- securing the home to the foundation
- connecting the utilities
- finishing installation
- doing the final inspection

Although most of the actual preparation and installation work will be done by professionals (usually employees or subcontractors working at the direction of the home dealer), you should be aware of the necessary procedures so that you will be able to oversee the installation and be sure that it is being properly executed. A home that is not properly supported and leveled can be seriously damaged, with ill-fitting doors and windows, cracked walls or ceilings, and buckled floors just some of the possible problems that can develop.

SITE PREPARATION

Before you can take delivery of your new home, you must be sure that the site has been properly prepared and that the site and foundation are ready to receive the home. If you intend to place the home on your own private site, you are responsible for preparing the site. Your dealer can advise you on how to prepare the site, or he can recommend a contractor to do the job. If you are renting or buying a site in a planned community, the dealer will usually arrange for the transportation, and the community manager will usually take care of site preparation. Before signing a lease for a community site, you should be sure that you understand their site preparation procedures and be aware of what the extra preparation and installation charges will be, if any.

If you are doing your own site preparation, you should ask the dealer, or whoever will install the home and warrant the installation, to inspect the work to be sure that everything has been properly prepared. Poor site or foundation preparation can mean delays in installing your home, and any delays can be very expensive when you are paying hourly rates for the truck and for members of the installation crew. Be sure the site and foundation are prepared so that there are no costly delays for the installation crew.

Although you may be able to do some of the site clearing work, work such as site grading and soil compaction (necessary to prevent the foundation from sinking or shifting on the earth fill) should be left to experts. Employing excavating experts will ensure that the site is graded so that surface water will drain away and the soil will be firm enough to support the weight of the home.

Things to remember regarding site preparation include:

- The site must have clear access routes so the delivery truck can reach the site and place the home.
- The site on which the foundation will sit must be level.
- The exact area where the home will sit should be free of surface debris such as rocks, trees, shrubs, and other vegetable matter (soil will settle when vegetable matter decays).
- The soil must be graded or sloped so that water will run away from the home on all four sides.
- The soil must be compacted, not loose, to ensure that the foundation will sit firm and level.

BUILDING THE FOUNDATION

In addition to fulfilling the dealer's specifications and meeting all local building code requirements, you should also investigate whether your mortgage company or rental community has any foundation requirements. Both the Federal Housing Administration (FHA) and the Veterans Administration (VA) have their own foundation requirements, so be sure that your foundation is in compliance with all codes to avoid needless hassles. Remind the contractor who will do your site preparation and foundation of what kind of financing you have, so he will know what the requirements are.

Foundation Considerations

If you will place your new home on your own property, you may be able to choose from a variety of foundation options. Foundations for manufactured homes vary from concrete slabs to full basements. Local codes will reflect such factors as soil type and climate. Your professional installer should know which foundations are required by local code and the demands of your financial institution.

If your home is set on a foundation that is not level, the structure can flex and twist, possibly causing poor window and door alignment, buckled floors, and even structural damage. Problems that are caused by improper leveling of the home will not be covered by your manufacturer's warranty, so be sure the home is leveled according to the manufacturer's instructions.

Checking for Level

Walk through the installed home before the installation crew leaves, and check to be sure the home is level. Take a carpenter's level along and check the floors in each room to be sure each floor is level. Signs that a home may not be level include windows or doors that bind and will not open or close easily, and closet, cabinet, or vanity doors that are obviously misaligned when you "eyeball" or visually inspect them. Have any problems with level corrected before the installation crew leaves the site.

Make Periodic Checks

Be aware that you must periodically recheck your manufactured home for level in the months following its placement. This periodic recheck is necessary because foundation support footings or piers can shift or settle and the foundation can become out of level. The Manufactured Housing Institute recommends that you recheck the level of your home sixty to ninety days following installation of the home, and once per year after that, to ensure that a level attitude is maintained and the structure of the home is not damaged.

ANCHORING YOUR HOME ON THE FOUNDATION

Because your home is both large and heavy, and because each side of the home is subjected to terrific pressure from wind loading, your house should be secured on its base or foundation by anchors. This anchoring will ensure that your home will not shift or become damaged, and it will help protect your home from damage from severe winds.

As with other steps in the home placement process, anchoring your home is a highly technical procedure, and must be done by a professional with a complete understanding of wind loads and stresses. It is not a do-it-yourself project. Ask your retail dealer for his recommendations, and be sure the person who does the anchoring project follows the manufacturer's recommendations that come with your home.

CONNECTING YOUR HOME TO UTILITIES

Be sure your contract for home installation includes having all the utilities connected. Ordinarily this utility hookup is not complicated, but it can become expensive if you have to call separate contractors to hook up each utility. Your home's electrical service must be hooked up to the power company lines; the sewer drain pipes from the home must be connected to municipal sewer lines or to your septic system; and water piping must be connected to the municipal water supply or to your own water well.

FINISHING

When your house has been secured and leveled on its foundation, you may have some finishing chores, such as installing a skirt or an enclosure around the foundation or doing the landscaping. If your home is installed in a community park, there may be park regulations to follow regarding landscaping. Certainly the increase in attention to finishing detail will improve the appearance of your site and provide added curb appeal for your own home.

If your home is a double-wide or multiple-unit home, there may be some work on the exterior to complete the siding where the units join together. There may also be some work on the interior of the home, installing molding and/or joining carpet where the two halves of the home meet.

As we mentioned elsewhere, if you install your home on your own property, and there are no other structures or trees nearby to shelter your home from the elements, you should consider planting several rows of evergreen trees to serve as a windbreak. Planting a windbreak can make your home more comfortable as well as reduce energy costs.

Siting a Garage or Shed

The Foremost Insurance Company survey shows that 59 percent of all manufactured home owners have garages or storage sheds on their sites. Before placing your home, plan where the garage will be located. If you can position the garage or shed so that the building shelters the home from prevailing winter winds, the extra building(s) can become a valuable aid in controlling energy costs.

USE YOUR INSTALLATION GUIDE

The foregoing information should help you in the task of getting your home placed on its new site. In addition to this information, you should receive an installation guide with your new home that will help you with any problems that may be peculiar to your particular home. Be sure you understand, however, that the information provided is not intended to help you do your own home installation. Home installation is a very technical business and should not be done by inexperienced people.

INSPECTING THE HOME

Now comes the day you have been waiting for: your home is installed on its own site and ready for you to move in. But before you pack your toothbrush, take a tour around the place and be sure everything is in order. The key is to find any problems at the earliest possible moment and to report the problems to the dealer or the installer well within the time limits of the warranty(s).

As noted earlier, it is a good idea to be present (but not in the way) during the installation of the home. Ask the installer to walk with you through the home and help you spot any potential problems. As you tour the home together, the installer will be able to answer any questions you may have.

What to Look for During Your Inspection

Open and close all interior and exterior doors, including the doors on closets, vanities, and cabinets. Do all doors open and close easily, without binding or rubbing on the floor or on jambs? Close the door. Inspect the crack between the door and its frame. Is the crack uniform in width, or is the crack wider in places, with the door rubbing against the frame in other places? Slight misalignment problems with doors may be due to minor hinge problems, or they may indicate twisting of the frames due to a home that is not level. Ask the installer to explain any apparent problems and to correct the problems before he leaves.

Check the entire home, both interior and exterior. Inspect all molding and trim. Do miter joints fit tightly, or are cracks apparent at the joints? Are any cracks or open joints due to poor workmanship in fitting the trim or molding, or is the home uneven, causing the joints to open up?

Do all toilets flush and all water faucets work? Is there hot water? Do all appliances operate properly, including the furnace and air conditioning? Are all moldings in place, carpets stretched tight and secured?

Are there any signs of transit damage either on the exterior siding and trim or on the interior?

Using the Manufacturer's Inspection Checklist

Most manufacturers include a inspection checklist in the owner's manual, and request that the owner complete the checklist and return it to the manufacturer as soon as possible. As you make your inspection, jot down every defect you see, regardless of how minor it may seem. Date the checklist and make multiple copies: one for your records, one for the manufacturer, and another for the dealer.

7

Barriers to Manufactured Housing

Because of economic factors and wartime shortages of building materials, virtually no residential housing was produced in the U.S. during the Depression decade of the 1930s or the war years of the first half of the 1940s. As the war ended and millions of GIs returned to civilian life, there was a great housing shortage, and the federal government turned its attention from war production to the housing industry. At that time, it was in the best interests of the entire nation to promote the housing industry, because we needed not only housing for our people but also the peace-time jobs the industry could generate.

New housing legislation created or expanded government-backed home financing in the form of the FHA (Federal Housing Administration) and GI loan programs. The federal government thus heavily subsidized home ownership. Because of government guarantees, the middle class could now buy a house with little or no down payment, and mortgage interest and property taxes were deductible on income taxes. Within a decade, the nation went from being a nation of renters (where one-third of families owned while two-thirds of families rented) to a nation in which two-thirds of families were home owners. Driven by these government programs and subsidies, we set out to house a nation.

A LESSON FROM HISTORY

Back in the late (post-World War II) 1940s, I started working with my father on housing projects. Our first efforts were building modest homes for returning GIs and for families left homeless by the Depression. The homes were small, about 24 feet x 32 feet, or 768 square feet. These were very basic houses: they had no garages, no carpeted floors, and no built-in appliances. Located in mid-America (Wichita, Kansas), these basic two-bedroom homes cost a total of less than $8,000.00, including the building site.

With that background in mind, you might imagine the shock with which I read today's housing ads, where houses costing well over $100,000.00 are listed as being "affordable." The fact of the matter is that today's average new house is 2,000 square feet and costs $148,800.00, well beyond the budget of the average wage-earner. At least one-third of our families cannot afford today's housing prices. To provide affordable housing for all, we must mount a campaign that equals the efforts of the post-war era.

HOUSING BARRIERS

Housing is such a basic human need that one might think it is in the best interests of all our citizens to see our population comfortably housed. The fact is that there are many powerful interests lobbying *against* acceptance of affordable housing. Some of the opposition is due to ignorance of manufactured housing on the part either of the general population or of elected officials. Some opposition is fueled by the "not in my back yard" syndrome — residents fear that the presence of manufactured homes may lower the resale value of their own homes, so they resist any intrusion of manufactured homes into their communities. Some opposition is from on-site builders, due to fear of sales competition from the less expensive manufactured housing.

In addition to direct opposition to manufactured homes, there is discrimination in financing rates, higher insurance premiums, and state and local taxation. In each case, representatives from government, financial, or insurance institutions can offer an explanation in defense of their own positions, but these explanations often will not stand much investigation.

Another serious barrier to affordable manufactured housing is the image that the public has of "mobile homes" and "mobile home parks." The manufactured home has been thought of as being the shape and color of a sardine can; the parks where they were sited are thought of as scraped cow pastures, devoid of trees or landscaping. Although both the appearance and siting of manufactured homes have changed tremendously, the negative image of the manufactured homes and the home parks has not changed as dramatically, and with some consumer education the negative images might be put to rest.

HOME APPEAL

Yesterday's mobile home parks were known for narrow trails that were often unpaved; high density, with homes crowded together on narrow lots; lack of garages or storage sheds, so each lot was cluttered; no skirting or landscape shrubbery around the base of the home; and a trailer hitch up front that suggested the occupant was one hour ahead of a posse and could move out at a moment's notice.

The home itself was a streamlined affair covered with aluminum and shaped to be aerodynamic, reminding one of the Nash Ambassador automobile of the 1950s. The aluminum was either painted with racing stripes or left as shiny as a fishing spoon. There was no mistaking this home for a vine-covered cottage: this was a horse of a different color.

Today, the mobile home has given way to the manufactured home. Exterior siding may be aluminum lap siding, vinyl, wood, or pre-finished steel. Windows may be either wood or vinyl, the same type of windows found in stick-built homes. Window options include skylights and bay or garden windows that let in sunshine and outdoors scenery.

The roofs of manufactured homes are no longer just flat and aluminum-clad. Depending on the type of home you select, the roof may be gabled, with asphalt shingles in your choice of colors and styles. In short, the manufactured home may look just like the home in which you grew up.

In addition to having a more traditional home appearance, the sited manufactured home today is set up with exterior amenities such as a carport or garage, a deck, a porch, and landscaping. Home surveys show that 80 percent of manufactured homes have unattached structures such as storage sheds, garages, or barns on their sites. These structures not only reduce clutter through added storage space, they also add to the curb appeal and provide a look of permanence to the site.

NATIONAL STANDARDS

Manufactured home construction is subject to a national code, as no other type of housing is. Manufactured homes built since September 15, 1976 conform to the National Manufactured Home Construction and Safety Standards established by the U.S. Congress. Because of these code standards, the strength, durability, and safety of the manufactured home are equal to that of a stick-built home.

SITE APPEAL

Almost two-thirds of all manufactured homes are sited in land-lease community developments or parks. Today's land-lease community bears little resemblance to the crowded parks of yesterday. Today's community development undergoes a lengthy process of planning, court proceedings, hearings with local governments, and referendums. Cooperation with building and zoning officials is required to achieve zoning changes that will permit manufactured housing. For example, many communities have gained local approval by restricting homes to multi-section or double-wide models that have a pitched roof and asphalt shingles. Those homes also are required to have lap-type siding, so that the exterior of the homes closely resembles site-built housing.

The typical land-lease community of today has an upgraded image. The entrance to the community may have an attractive entrance sign and professional landscaping. Streets are wide and paved, often curving to avoid the "little metal boxes" appearance of straight streets and straight rows of homes. Mature trees provide both an attractive appearance and summer shade/winter shelter. Off-street parking, often in garages or carports, also adds to the cleaner image of the new community. Landscaping berms along streets provide a double benefit of being a buffer against traffic for residents and adding visual enhancement.

Manufactured home communities often are required by local code to build recreational areas for residents, whereas the site-built home builder usually contributes only to area or municipal facilities. Tennis courts, club houses, wetland preserves with ponds or lakes, swimming pools, and playground equipment are other amenities commonly found in manufactured home communities.

Homes are often arranged in a cluster-type plan that increases privacy while providing easy pedestrian access to park or wetland jogging/walking paths. Lot sizes are being increased, offering both enhanced privacy for residents and a more appealing, less cluttered community appearance. For example, the Shelby West community in suburban Detroit, Michigan has sites that are 52 feet x 85 feet, or a total of 4,420 square feet. Larger lots add to curb appeal by reducing the density of the sites plus providing landscaped "green" areas between the homes.

In the past, the cluttered, transient appearance of mobile home parks made them a target for zoning discrimination by communities. In solving the Catch-22 of making manufactured housing more accept-able to the communities, cooperation is needed between the builder/developer and the various teams he employs and the local city or township officials.

INSURANCE

Owners of manufactured homes pay higher casualty insurance premiums, often as much as 30 percent higher, than do the owners of site-built homes. The attitude of the insurance industry in the past was that the manufactured home suffered higher casualty losses — for fire, storm damage, etc. — than site-built homes did, and therefore should pay a higher insurance premium. But a survey conducted by Foremost Insurance Company, a large insurer of manufactured homes, shows that manufactured homes actually have *less* casualty loss than does site-built housing. Manufactured home dealers complain that, even with evidence pointing to the contrary, manufactured home owners still pay higher insurance premiums per thousand dollars of valuation than do their neighbors with site-built housing. Before they are regulated by the government into doing so, the insurance industry should remove such barriers to affordable housing, and make insurance premiums for manufactured homes comparable to those for site-built homes. If they fail to do so, agencies such as HUD may mandate more equitable insurance treatment.

HOME FINANCING

According to surveys, 65 percent of manufactured home buyers finance their purchases via a mortgage. But for loan purposes, manufactured homes are often viewed as chattel property rather than as real estate, and buyers often pay a higher interest rate on the loan than they would pay if buying a site-built home.

One officer of a financial institution told us a manufactured home that is set atop a permanent foundation is viewed as real estate, while any home left on its wheels would be viewed as chattel property and would pay a higher loan interest rate. Although many manufactured homes are financed with FHA loans, the home buyer still commonly pays a higher interest rate than he would pay when buying a site-built home with an FHA mortgage. Thus, unequal mortgage interest rates are an obvious financial barrier to affordable housing.

Comparing Costs

To compare financing costs, consider that a personal property loan may require a 15 percent down payment, and cost 13.5 APR (annual percentage rate) when financed over twenty years. A home financed with conventional mortgage insurance may require a 10 percent down payment, cost 9.5 APR, and cover a thirty-year term.

Housing officials point out that a mortgage is a mortgage is a mortgage: i.e., any mortgage requires about the same amount of time and expense to service as any other mortgage. Obviously, a $30,000.00 mortgage on a manufactured home would not produce as much income for the financial institution as would a $100,000.00 mortgage on a site-built home. There should be a way to pool mortgages on manufactured homes so that the buyer is not penalized.

Low Repossession and Delinquency Rates

Another question on the subject of mortgage parity is the question of delinquencies and repossessions for manufactured homes. According to the American Banking Association Consumer Credit Delinquency Bulletin, manufactured home loans that were more than thirty days past due averaged about three percent of loans outstanding for 1991. But the number of manufactured home loan repossessions per 1,000 loans outstanding was slightly under two (see chart). These figures are not excessive and should not be seen as justifying higher rates for mortgage interest. It would appear that default and repossession rates for manufactured homes are no worse than those for site-built homes.

DEPRECIATION?

Contrary to what may be popular belief, manufactured homes do not experience rapid depreciation in

value. In fact, in a study of four southern California communities, manufactured home appreciation increased faster than that for comparable site-built homes in three out of the four communities. The study, done by Tony Hadley of the California Manufactured Housing Institute (CMHI), included only manufactured homes that were double-wide, single-family, and affixed to foundations. The sites were fee simple property, meaning that the land was sold with the home, so the home packages are comparable to site-built homes. The study shows that manufactured homes rose in value at an average annual rate of 8.17 percent to 17.5 percent, in a five-year (1984-89) period. This means that manufactured homes appreciated at a rate 4 to 20 percent higher than for neighboring site-built, single-family homes.

Viewing Manufactured Homes as Real Estate

Actually, studies done by Foremost Insurance Company in 1980 revealed that, beginning in 1970, manufactured housing had appreciated at a rate of about five percent per year. Prior to that time, the theory of manufactured home depreciation was chiefly due to the practice of licensing the homes as vehicles, and applying depreciation schedules to them in much the same way that automobiles are depreciated. This practice was so extensive that "blue books" were used to determine the value of a manufactured home, just as the blue book is the standard reference for automobile value estimates. As manufactured homes begin to be viewed as real estate, the mindset of attributing high depreciation to them will cease. Rather than using depreciation tables when assessing the value of manufactured homes, appraisers now consider factors such as replacement costs, location, size (total floor space), and marketability, just as they would in assessing the value of site-built homes.

FIVE FACTORS AFFECTING VALUE

Manufactured Housing Quarterly magazine (Fall/Winter 1991) cites five factors that affect values for manufactured homes. These factors are quality, location, demand, size, and appearance. Here is a review of each of these factors, as seen by *MHQ* magazine.

Quality

As noted elsewhere, manufactured home construction standards equal or exceed the standards established for site-built homes. National standards have been in place since 1976, so even older manufactured homes — up to seventeen years old — meet these standards. Efficiencies of factory construction make it possible to build homes of equal or greater durability and safety, while reducing construction costs by as much as 30 percent when compared to site-built homes.

Location

Also in the early 1970s, higher development standards for manufactured home communities were adopted. Today's standards permit six to eight home sites per acre, as compared to the ten to twelve site per acre density of the past. The lower density standards per acre for manufactured homes compare with density standards for condominium development. Planned manufactured home communities also now include recreational facilities, swimming pools, and nature parks. This upgrading of development standards in turn has led to greater approval of community development in traditional residential areas, so manufactured homes are no longer stuck in undesirable land parcels. The old saw about the three most important factors in home resale value being location, location, and location is true. As better locations become available for manufactured homes, their resale values rise.

Demand

Better locations increase demand and resale value of manufactured homes, as stated above. But another important factor in manufactured home value appreciation has been the tremendous inflation in the cost of single-family, site-built homes. The rapid increase in home prices has moderated somewhat in recent years as the overall inflation rate has fallen. Even so, as stated elsewhere, the average site-built home sale price reached $148,800.00 in 1989. When the nation has a situation in which the average family cannot afford the average home, alternatives must be found for affordable housing, and demand for manufactured homes is sure to rise.

Size

The size of manufactured homes has been increasing, as buyers move toward purchase of double-wide or multiple unit housing. Manufactured homes are now available in sizes ranging from 1,000 square feet to 2,500 square feet. In addition to any increase in the actual floor space of the homes are the pluses of amenities such as decks, porches, and garages to improve the liveability and appearance of the homes. More and larger windows, skylights, and patio doors also bring the outdoors in, and make the homes seem roomier.

Appearance

Yet another factor in the area of demand is the improved appearance or curb appeal of the manufactured homes. Their larger size, gabled roof lines, and conventional exterior finishes such as asphalt roof shingles and aluminum, wood, or vinyl siding all contribute to home value appreciation. Addition of garages, storage sheds, decks, and foundations or foundation skirting also help anchor the homes on their sites and make the homes seem more conventional.

WHY THE BARRIERS?

As one ponders the barriers that have held back the development of more affordable housing, it becomes clear that the largest barriers to overcome are those of *image* and *regulation*. Many people, including local officials, have never surveyed a planned community of manufactured homes, but instead harbor the old images of transient people, unruly children, and unattractive mobile homes set atop concrete blocks in mobile home parks.

Media images serve only to fuel the fire: who has not seen the TV news coverage of a manufactured home community that has been devastated by a tornado or a hurricane? Yet video footage of storm damage to site-built homes would reveal comparable home damage.

Along with the negative image of manufactured homes has been the discriminatory attitude of local and state officials. Consider that until passage of The Fair Housing Act of 1988, local restrictive covenants in many areas excluded families with children from living in manufactured homes. Today, such restrictions are illegal.

There is a lengthy list of regulations that drive up the cost of housing, both site-built and manufactured. Many or most of those regulations would not stand scrutiny if they were examined in court. They were passed by local politicos who defended their actions with claims of "protecting [their own] home resale values," or "necessary for the public safety."

In Your Community
How interested is your own community in removing barriers to affordable housing? Consider that state and local governments tax any home from the day you apply for a building permit. Charges for fees and permits associated with the home can be prohibitive and can vary widely by region. Consider that many or most states levy a sales tax on building materials (for either site-built or manufactured homes) and then levy property taxes against the home the minute it is finished, to be exacted annually, forever. In some states, there is also a sales tax on the price of the finished manufactured home: Minnesota, my state, levies a sales tax on 65 percent of the home's selling price. Consider also that sales taxes are levied on building materials bought for home maintenance and repair. In my own state of Minnesota, the tree-trimming crew handed me a bill for $340.00 (labor only) to trim my trees, then added 6.5 percent state sales tax to that bill. Can one wonder why we see so much neglected property about, considering how our state governments penalize any effort at home maintenance by taxing the building materials and necessary tools, and by increasing the property taxes for even modest home improvements?

The Myth of Protecting Property Values
Often, the citizenry (us) approves of (or at least does not actively oppose) exclusionary housing legislation, on the grounds of simply protecting property values. In most or many cases that is not true, and even if true, the restrictions are at least undemocratic and at worst are unconstitutional. Further, discrimination against affordable housing may be seen to harm only *them*, but in fact the *them* we are excluding with our barriers includes our own children and retired parents.

8
Community Development

Across the nation, home communities that have been developed and operated successfully are demonstrating that the solution to our affordable housing dilemma can be found in manufactured housing. As local governments, builders, developers, and manufacturers begin to cooperate, they are finding that manufactured housing can be handled so it is an asset to the community. In fact, manufactured housing may likely prove to be the *only* viable solution to housing all our citizens. Tony Hadley, Director of Local Government and Development Services for the California Manufactured Housing Institute, in an article that appeared in the *Manufactured Housing Quarterly* (*MHQ*, Summer 1991), notes that new zoning laws enacted in California benefit "first-time home buyers, single parents, retirees, immigrants and farm families" the most.

FOLLOWING THE CALIFORNIA EXAMPLE

All communities should support less discriminatory zoning laws because most of us have family members who belong to one or more of these groups. We should also note here that the article quoted states that none of the negative consequences that were predicted by critics came true: there has been no reduction in property value for existing community homes, no overwhelming of exclusive neighborhoods with sub-standard homes, no problems that prevented local government agencies from enforcing appropriate ordinances to ensure community health, welfare, or safety standards. The California experience is helping to prove that not only are many zoning laws found to be unconstitutional when they are tested in court, but protests and

objections that seek to exclude or ban manufactured housing are without merit. Hadley points out that the key is to encourage local governments to regulate, but not to ban, manufactured housing.

Following are a few examples, taken at random, of successful execution of community developments. The examples are taken from success stories that have appeared in *Manufactured Housing Quarterly* magazine.

KING COUNTY (SEATTLE), WASHINGTON

In the 1980s, the King County (Washington) Housing Authority began to develop manufactured housing to fill the void for affordable housing in that area (twenty-five miles from Seattle, WA). So in the spring of 1991, when New Pacific Development decided to sell a nearly-completed 148-home community, the Housing Authority asked the King County government to grant a low-interest loan to acquire the project and complete the development. Further financing was obtained from the U.S. Bank of Washington. Market surveys done at the time showed there was a great demand for low- to middle-income housing in that area.

The King County Housing Authority teamed up with Puget Power, the local electrical company, to explore the possibility of filling the project with homes that met strict energy standards. The Moduline International company agreed to supply the homes, which would meet both Bonneville Power's Super Good Cents and Puget Power's Comfort Plus energy specifications. These specifications include energy-efficient vinyl windows, R-

33 insulation in the ceilings, R-30 insulation in the floors, and R-19 insulation in the walls. The 148-home development was scheduled to be completed in one year, by April of 1992.

The housing project, called Glenbrook, offers homes that have 1,200 square feet to 1,400 square feet of floor space, including three bedrooms and two baths, and cost between $76,000.00 and $89,000.00. The price includes both the home and the lot, and no-down-payment financing is provided via a condominium lease-purchase program. These prices compare with site-built homes of similar size that cost a minimum of $125,000.00 — and up. The cost advantage difference of $29,000.00 to $36,000.00 over comparable site-built homes provides an obvious advantage in affordability to mid-income buyers.

And Glenbrook is no ugly-duckling development. The homes are set atop permanent foundations, on lots that are attractively landscaped. The roofs are gabled and shingled, and covered carports plus concrete driveways and walks complete the picture. The view from the picture windows includes Mount Rainier and/or open wetlands scenery.

SHELBY TOWNSHIP (DETROIT), MICHIGAN

The development of manufactured home communities in Shelby Township (north of Detroit, Michigan) started with a 625-space project called Shelby Forest. The project is called a "land-lease manufactured housing community," which means that residents purchase the homes but make monthly lease payments on the sites. Not having to buy the lot reduces the total price, and therefore reduces the down payment for the homes.

The Shelby Forest development was an immediate success, for several reasons. The first reason was that it filled an obvious need for affordable housing. But a second reason for the success is that a great deal of prior planning and cooperation went into the development. The community is attractively landscaped and has a club house and pool. The homes, both single-wide and multi-section, have gabled

roofs with asphalt shingles, as well as lap siding similar to that of any site-built home. These features provide exterior appeal and help to avoid any stigma of having a "manufactured home" look. Even so, the project was approved only after a drawn-out process that included hearings, court action, and referendums. Eventually, the first community was successfully completed and occupied, and attention was turned to developing another community, on land that was just one mile to the west.

Shelby West

The second development, Shelby West, was built on a ninety-eight-acre plot. Because of the initial success with Shelby Forest, the land for Shelby West had already been zoned for manufactured homes. Approval for the site plan was obtained more easily because developers agreed to bring in only manufactured homes that closely resembled ordinary site-built homes: all the homes in Shelby West are multi-section units and have gabled and shingled roofs and lap siding. Also, all the homes include decks, porches, carports, and landscaping to further increase the curb appeal.

A model home area, which was assembled by three home dealers and showcased twenty-eight different homes, helped to fill the development quickly. A well-planned media sales campaign, waged by the developer and the dealers, resulted in having many of the homes pre-sold before the project's official opening day.

The development planning for Shelby West was not without problems. A portion of the ninety-eight-acre parcel contains wetlands that are regulated by both the state and federal governments. Consultations and negotiations were necessary with both the state of Michigan's Department of Natural Resources and the U.S. Army Corps of Engineers. In the final decision, nearly thirty acres of the ninety-eight-acre parcel were set aside as a wetland preserve, and a five-acre lake was created as part of the settlement.

In spite of losing nearly one-third of the total area to wetland preservation, the final community consists of a cluster-type plan with a total of 461 lots. The lots are 52 feet by 85 feet and contain an average of 4,420 square feet of area. The community center, pool, and common parking take up less than one acre. The homes in Shelby West cost between $35,000.00 and $45,000.00 — very affordable homes when one considers their being sited in a major metropolitan area.

The entrance of the home community is marked with an attractive sign and is attractively landscaped. Donald Westphal, ASLA, a landscape architect with twenty-five years of experience in planning manufactured home communities (and author of the *MHQ* story), points out that a professional landscape plan is important because it not only enhances the appeal of the park entry, but it also motivates community residents to cooperate by keeping their own lots well groomed through the years. As landscaping matures and trees or shrubs fill in, there is an increasing positive effect on the "curb appeal" of the home site.

OPENING UP RESIDENTIAL LOTS

In 1989, the legislature of the state of California passed the Fair Zoning Legislation, which decreed that manufactured homes could be sited on any single residential building lot. This action ended the practice of shunting manufactured homes to undesirable lots, or banning them altogether, and opened up thousands of residential building lots for occupancy by manufactured homes. Tony Hadley, Director of the California Manufactured Housing Institute, writes in *MHQ* that, because of the new legislation, "Local officials have discovered a number of effective, yet fair, regulatory tools that ensure the compatibility of manufactured homes in existing neighborhoods."

Hadley also points out that, as regulations against manufactured housing development have been eliminated, there have been reciprocal efforts by home manufacturers to design housing that is attractive and that blends into home sites located in the midst of conventional housing. This improved image for manufactured housing in turn reduces the friction between local government housing officials, area residents, and developers of manufactured housing, and eases the resistance once encountered by this type of housing. This reduction in confrontation between the various community factions can help to end the chicken-or-the-egg, Catch-22 problem that said: we won't include you because you don't fit in; we don't fit in because you exclude us.

Eliminating Zoning Restrictions

One facet of the Catch-22 roadblock has been the inability of public-sector redevelopment officials to utilize manufactured housing while the zoning restrictions remained. With such zoning restrictions ended, these government agencies can move on with the job of supplying affordable housing for all citizens. The savings in tax money made possible by government's utilization of manufactured housing should also appeal to the overburdened taxpayer who must pay for public housing programs.

This move toward increased cooperation is beginning to pay off, although the necessary changes will not take place overnight. Old attitudes and business practices die hard, and further patience and cooperation are needed in order for the Fair Zoning legislation to become a complete reality. Still, the California Fair Zoning legislation should serve as a guideline to other state and local officials to reform their antiquated and discriminatory zoning laws, so that affordable housing becomes a reality. To loosely quote Supreme Court Justice Potter Stewart in his opinion on open housing for all, if we cannot say that every citizen is entitled to access to affordable housing, then the Constitution has made a promise that we cannot keep.

AFFORDABILITY ANALYSIS
IMPACT OF SUBSIDIES

Prepared for: The City of Petaluma, August 26, 1991

MANUFACTURED HOUSING

	SALES PRICE	Household Income to Qualify	% of Median Income	Down-payment	Monthly Housing Expense
NO SUBSIDY	99,050	33,636	78%	4,953	925
FEE SUBSIDY	91,550	31,127	73%	4,578	856
LAND SUBSIDY	74,050	25,273	59%	3,703	695
LAND & FEE SUBSIDY	66,550	22,764	53%	3,328	626

STICK BUILT

	SALES PRICE	Household Income to Qualify	% of Median Income	Down-payment	Monthly Housing Expense
NO SUBSIDY	114,650	38,836	91%	5,733	1,068
FEE SUBSIDY	107,150	36,335	85%	5,358	999
LAND SUBSIDY	89,650	30,479	71%	4,483	838
LAND & FEE SUBSIDY	82,150	27,975	65%	4,108	769

IMPORTANT REFERENCE NOTES: The accompanying Notes and Assumptions are an integral part of this Schedule. Monthly housing expense assumes payment of: loan of 5% down at 10% fixed rate, and a 30 year amortization; insurance; and taxes. Household income to qualify assumes 33% of family income for monthly housing expense.

Information courtesy of Farr Consulting Group.

COMPONENTS OF SALES PRICE AND MONTHLY HOUSING EXPENSE

Sales Price Comparison	Stick Built including Land	Manufactured including Land
Dwelling	$60,950	49,550
Land	25,000	25,000
Developer Financing	5,700	1,500
City Fees	7,500	7,500
Developer Overhead and Management	15,500	13,000
Marketing	2,500	2,500
Projected Sales Price	$114,650	$99,050

Monthly Housing Expense

Loan Payment (5% down, 10% interest, 30 years)	948	819
Insurance	15	15
Property Taxes (1.10%)	105	91
Total Monthly Housing Expense	$ 1,068	925
Household Income Required	**$ 38,836**	**$ 33,636**
Percent of Median Household Income	**91%**	**78%**
Median Household Income for Sonoma County	**42,900**	**42,900**

MANUFACTURED HOUSING
14% Less cost to purchase including land
13% Lower monthly cost
Require NO subsidies to attain affordability
More households can qualify for a home loan

Information courtesy of Farr Consulting Group.

DWELLING COST COMPARISON —STICK BUILT

Comparison Cost (dwelling fully equipped, sited, fenced, and landscaped)

	Dwelling		$ 60,950
	Per Square Foot		$ 48.76
Basic Unit			
	Dwelling Construction (incl. garage and foundation)	$ 54,700	
	Architectural	3,500	
Subtotal			58,200
Additional Site Work			
	Underground	600	
Subtotal			600
Finish Work (common to all)			
	Driveway & Walks ($2.50 sq. ft.)	900	
	Landscaping (front)	750	
	Fencing ($6 L.F.)	500	
Subtotal			2,150
TOTAL DWELLING COST			$60,950

NOTES: Cost per square foot is calculated by dividing total sited dwelling cost by total average floor space of home including garage, or $60,950/1250. The unit cost is approximately $48.76/sq. ft. for a stick-built dwelling, ready to occupy.

DWELLING COST COMPARISON —MANUFACTURED HOUSING

1250 Sq. Ft. Home, 2-Car Garage, Ready to Occupy

Comparison Cost (dwelling fully equipped, sited, fenced, and landscaped)

	Dwelling		$ 49,550
	Per Square Foot		$ 39.64
Basic Unit			
	Factory Invoice (includes all appliances, carpeting, fixtures)	$ 36,250	
	Transportation	1,200	
	Setup: connect, install carpet, tape, and texture	2,000	
Total for home, delivered and installed			39,450
Plus Siting & Site Construction			
	Underground	600	
	Foundation ($20 L.F. perimeter wall and I-beam support system)	3,000	
	Garage (includes slab, framing, siding, garage door, Sheetrock on firewall only)	6,500	
Subtotal			10,100
Finish Work (common to all)			
	Driveway & Walks ($2.50 sq. ft.)	900	
	Landscaping (front)	750	
	Fencing ($6 L.F.)	500	
Subtotal			2,150
TOTAL DWELLING COST			$49,550

NOTES: A manufactured home costs approximately 19% less than a comparable stick-built dwelling. Cost per square foot is calculated by dividing total sited dwelling cost by total average floor space of home with garage, or $49,550/1250. The unit cost is approximately $39.64/sq. ft. for a manufactured home, ready to occupy.

Information provided by Farr Consulting Group, 23 Ross Common, P.O. Box 475, Ross, CA 94957.

9
Manufactured Housing Options

The term "manufactured housing" may include that group of homes that are completely built in the factory and delivered as a finished product on their own steel frame and wheels. These homes were formerly called "mobile homes," but the name was officially changed to manufactured homes. Similar to the manufactured home is the *modular home*. Like manufactured homes, these, too, are completely assembled and finished in a factory. Modular homes are sometimes built in sections, but are built on a wooden floor structure and are loaded onto a low-boy type trailer for transport to the final site. Although there are other types of home that are generally grouped under the name of "manufactured homes," the Manufactured Housing Institute represents only these two types of housing — manufactured homes and modular homes — built in a factory and delivered as a complete home package to a site. Other factory-built homes may include panelized homes, pre-cut homes, and log and timber homes.

In this book, we have concentrated on manufactured homes as the affordable alternative to site-built homes. Although modular homes are also covered under the MHI banner, the production of modular housing has been small, and the total number of modular homes built fell from a high of 29,567 units in 1987 to 26,118 homes in 1989. The state of Pennsylvania alone accounted for more than one-third of the modular home production with 9,800 units produced in 1989. Residential modular home consumption accounted for only 2 percent of

all housing permits nationally in 1989, while manufactured homes accounted for 14 percent of all home building permits for 1989.

In this chapter, we will review all the various types of homes that are loosely included under the name of "manufactured homes." In this discussion, we will take the wider view that any home that is completely or partially fabricated in a factory is a manufactured home, and deserves consideration in our quest for affordable alternatives to traditional stick-built housing.

MODULAR HOMES

Back in the early 1970s, the Nixon Administration ordered a new housing study that was called "Operation Breakthrough." The object of the study was to find ways to solve the problem of affordable housing by mass-producing homes in factories. Many of the largest and best-known building materials and home appliance corporations joined in the study to find ways to produce housing that was affordable because of the efficiencies possible with factory production. The results of that study were less than encouraging.

There was no "breakthrough" in affordable housing from Operation Breakthrough. One of the drawbacks of modular housing was that extra strength was built into the units to withstand the stress of moving them to their site. This added structural strength cost money and increased the cost of the home. However, the added strength of the home was of no value once the modular house was positioned on site and was no longer subject to moving stresses.

What the industry did learn from the Operation Breakthrough study was that many of the factors that increased the cost of a home were outside the possible savings that could be accomplished by factory efficiencies. True, some economies were accomplished by setting up production lines for assembling home components. But this was not where the bulk of the housing expense arose, and no amount of factory efficiency could overcome the fixed costs that are generated at the building site. These fixed costs apply to any home, whether factory-built or site-built, and are beyond remedy through any savings of materials or labor. Only manufactured homes, formerly known as mobile homes, escape some or most of those on-site costs.

Part of the economy of manufactured homes is due to reduction in actual building costs because of factory production; manufactured houses cost about half as much to build ($24.17 per square foot for a multi-section home) as a site-built home ($53.25 per square foot). Another source of economy is that the manufactured homes are completely finished at the factory, and require only minimal on-site labor (leveling the home on the foundation, plus utility hookup) before being occupied. Because labor costs vary greatly by region, differences in local labor costs can be responsible for a wide variation between the prices of site-built homes. The final cost savings for manufactured homes is due to the fact that they can be sited in land-lease communities where the costs of land and utility services are included in monthly lease fees, and therefore do not have to be paid by the home buyer.

Government Costs

When you start to build a house on site, you must go through a lengthy process of dealing with local governments. You must have plans drawn and must pay for building permits and inspection fees. By some industry estimates, the cost of government regulation of housing can add from 20 percent to 35 percent to the total cost of the home. The economies of factory production cannot reduce or control this portion of the home's cost.

Government's role in the building of a home is not limited to just the cost of the building permits and inspections; it goes far beyond those more obvious costs. There are charges for installation of water and sewerage services; there may be sales taxes on all or part of the building materials at construction time, plus sales taxes on any materials bought in the future for maintenance or repair. There are property taxes to pay for schools, roads, and fire and police service. Some of these costs are, of course, justified, but there are many bureaucratic rules in the building codes that add to the cost of the home without any benefit or justification whatsoever.

The Bureaucracy at Work

Let me illustrate this point with a few examples of totally unjustified and arbitrary rules I have encountered personally as a contractor. At one time, the electrical utility company in my city was pushing for the expansion of electric heating of homes. I helped build several of these all-electric homes.

In one suburb of Minneapolis, we ran afoul of the local building inspector. As he strolled around the exterior of the house, his attention went to the roof, which did not have a protruding chimney pipe. "Where is the chimney?" he demanded. We explained to the inspector that the house would have electric resistance heating. There would be no furnace and therefore no combustion. One of the economies of electric resistance heating was that you did not have to pay for a chimney. "But," the inspector rebutted, "The building code of the city requires a chimney. You've got to install a chimney before I'll sign off on the permit." No matter how we argued, no matter the pure reasoning behind our protestations, this petty official stood firm. No chimney, no permit.

You cannot delay these things forever, if you want to make a living. We paid $125.00 for a metal chimney, cut holes from the basement through the floor, through the roof, and flashed the chimney atop the roof. In the basement, we built a cradle of

2 x 4s to hold the chimney up, there being no furnace to which to connect the chimney. Hundreds of dollars were wasted to satisfy this inspector, in a time when hundreds of dollars was a lot more money than it is today.

Another example of inspector stupidity? I owned a home in yet another Minneapolis suburb. The home was built in the mid-1960s, when no sewerage or water utilities were available in the area. All the houses had their own private wells and septic systems.

There came the day when municipal water and sewer lines were installed, and I could hook up to the city services. I went to city hall to obtain a permit, and found to my complete astonishment that the city codes decreed that the water service pipes be expensive copper, and the sewer drain pipes were to be cast iron, much more expensive than plastic drain pipe. I proposed to the plumbing inspector that I would install plastic piping, both for water supply and for sewer drains. Well, then, he sneered, he would not permit me to hook onto the municipal pipes.

Now you must understand that at that particular time they were installing all-plastic piping in the communities all around mine. One mile to the north of my house, in another city, they were installing the cheaper (and better, because plastic does not corrode) plastic water and sewer pipe. Why should I be made to pay for the more costly pipe?

I called the state code office. No, the state inspector assured me, they can't do that. The local city code cannot supersede the state code: the state code *was* the building code, and the state code permitted the use of plastic. This I reported to the local plumbing inspector, and again he repeated: no copper and cast iron pipe, no hookup to the services.

Now, you might wonder again whether I was right. The clincher was that the municipal piping in the streets was *plastic*. This petty dictator was requiring residents in this one small city to use copper and cast iron pipe to hook our houses to the *plastic* city

mains! How can you win? I didn't: in the end, it was go through a lengthy fight, or pay several hundred dollars extra for pipe to comply with totally ridiculous demands. I paid. So much for your friendly government offices.

Site Costs

Aside from the tribute extracted by government officials, there are other costs that are beyond remedy via factory housing. The increase in cost of building sites alone far outstripped the inflation of housing prices. Land prices in my suburb went from $1,000.00 for a half-acre site in the early 1960s to $30,000.00 or more for the same site by 1990. These price increases are beyond remedy, and the fact that you can place a manufactured home on a leased site is one of the prime economies possible with this type of housing.

There are other major expenses associated with the home site, and these too are difficult to control. One of these major costs is grading and excavating for a foundation or basement. Depending on the lay of the site, these excavating costs can easily add thousands of dollars to the house price. Other expenses include ditch excavation and piping to connect the water and sewer drain pipes to the house.

Masonry costs can also run up the final cost of the home. These costs are for laying block or pouring concrete basement walls, pouring the basement floor, and any chimney work for fireplaces. In addition, placing and finishing concrete floors in the garage, and pouring driveways, walks, and steps or porches can all add up to thousands of dollars more. These costs apply no matter how your house is built, whether on site or in a factory.

Planting a lawn, tree placement or removal, and other landscaping costs are costs that can contribute much to the final price of housing, and which cannot be alleviated by economies of factory construction. Before you consider any form of housing, be sure that you have counted in all these costs, all of which are variable only by region but are pretty much fixed by geographical area.

PANELIZED OR PRE-CUT HOMES

A panelized home is one in which the components are assembled into panels, or segments, of the roof, walls, or floor at a factory, and the panels are shipped to the job site for assembly. The panels may be complete, with framing, insulation, wallboard, and exterior sheathing and siding in place. In most cases, all the plumbing pipes and electrical wires are also in place. The panels can be assembled fairly quickly, reducing on-site labor, but you may need a crane to lift the panels into position, and it may require a trained crew to erect the panels and join them properly.

Pre-cut homes are sold as a kit with all the components cut to fit, and all the pieces ready for assembly. The main advantage for the do-it-yourself homeowner is that all the math and cutting angles are figured for him, so he is spared making any mistakes in cutting joists, rafters, or studs.

Take Site Costs into Consideration

Before considering building a panelized or pre-cut home, be sure you consider all the costs that are mentioned in Site Costs above. Although some sort of home kit package may sound reasonable in price, it does not include all the added expenses you will have at the site. Do not let an overzealous salesperson underestimate the additional costs you will incur for the lot, excavation, landscaping, masonry work, and the rest.

Time and "Sweat Equity"

Another common problem in building panelized or pre-cut home kits is to underestimate the amount of time it will take, and to overestimate the amount of work the buyer can do himself — and the possible savings from this "sweat equity." No matter what anyone tells you, not everyone can build his or her own house. It is a wiser and happier person who can take a realistic look at his own abilities and time available, and accurately decide just what he is capable of and what work should be left to professionals. Building a house involves putting in hundreds of hours of labor, even for an experienced person, and not everyone has enough free time to do

the job in a workmanlike manner. Building a house on weekends can easily stretch out to take up a hundred or more weekends, and the novice builder is sure to tire of his "bargain."

The pre-cut home is in actuality little more than a pile of lumber, cut to exact size. The cutting is not that much of a factor, in these days when all houses are built from assembled components such as pre-hung doors and roof trusses. Pre-cut home packages are becoming more rare as more components, such as roof trusses, become common.

LOG AND TIMBER HOMES

Log homes and timber-framed homes are offered as kits with all pieces cut and fit at the factory. All the pieces are numbered or coded to match together. Neither of these types of home is a candidate for do-it-yourself assembly, nor are these homes generally considered in the "affordable" bracket. Although they are beautiful and much in demand (last year over 1,000 log homes were shipped to Japan), they are strictly upper bracket and are not in competition for affordability. They also are not candidates for do-it-yourself assembly, so no labor savings are possible.

CONCLUSION

Of all the factory-built housing, only manufactured homes can be considered to be affordable alternatives to site-built homes. The obvious advantages are that the manufactured homes are delivered in completely finished trim and are ready for occupancy with only a minimum of on-site labor. When delivered to a community site, with land-lease provisions, there can be a small monthly rental fee for the site. Land and development costs are eliminated, so all the extra costs of site-built housing are avoided.

In addition, there are economies available from factory construction. Manufactured homes can be built for about one-half the per-square-foot cost of site-built homes. There is no doubt that manufactured homes will be the alternative choice to site-built homes as we seek to solve the affordability problem.

10
Summary and Checklists

The Manufactured Housing Institute provides a consumer's checklist in their brochure, "How to Buy a Manufactured Home." Following is a slightly abridged version of that summary and suggested checklist. We urge that you read and use the checklist to be sure you have overlooked nothing, and to make your shopping and buying experience as pleasant and trouble-free as possible. Remember, it is much easier, as well as less frustrating, to try to anticipate potential problems and to deal with them before they arise.

WARRANTY PROTECTION

❑ Check warranty protection offered by the home manufacturer, the retail dealer, the transporter, the installer, and all appliance manufacturers.

❑ Get all warranties in writing — verbal warranties are impossible to enforce.

❑ Understand that manufacturers' warranties do not apply for damages caused by faulty installation or owner's negligence, or for unauthorized repairs.

❑ Who performs the service covered by each of the warranties?

❑ Have you created a file containing all the warranties and other papers from your home purchase, and positioned the file for easy retrieval if any questions or problems arise?

PLACING YOUR HOME

❑ If you own your own land, have you checked for zoning regulations or restrictive covenants that prohibit placement of a manufactured home?

❑ Are utility services, including electric, gas, water, and sewerage lines, available to your home site, or will you have to pay extra to have these lines extended to your site?

❑ If it is impossible to extend utility lines — gas, water, and sewerage — to your property, is it economically feasible to build or install optional utility systems, such as propane (tank) gas, septic system for sewerage, and well water supplies?

❑ If you will locate your home in a planned community rental park, who will be responsible for grounds maintenance, snow plowing, and trash/garbage pickup? Are there grounds fees or other charges not covered by the monthly rental?

CHOOSING YOUR HOME

❑ What appearance or look do you want for the exterior of your manufactured home?

❑ What size home, in terms of floor space, number of bedrooms, etc., do you want or need?

❑ Have you checked state laws on transporting oversized loads (your own state, or any state you might move through) that might prevent you from moving your home?

❏ What custom options and features are available from your dealer?

❏ What appliance packages are available, and do the appliances have high energy efficiency ratings?

❏ What energy-saving options are available for your home?

INSTALLING YOUR HOME

❏ Who will inspect your home site prior to installation, to ensure that the site has been properly prepared?

❏ Is your site accessible by trucks transporting your home? (For example, a narrow lane between rows of trees on a wooded lot can be a complete barrier to home delivery.)

❏ Who will transport the home to the site? Is the cost of transportation included in the price of the home?

❏ Does the transporting company provide a written warranty for any damage that occurs during transporting?

❏ What foundation options are available, and what are required by local codes or financial companies?

❏ Does the transporter/dealer supply an experienced installation crew to be sure the home is properly leveled and secured to the foundation?

❏ What landscaping or other finishing touches will be needed?

❏ Who will secure the utility connections? (In some instances, the installer will connect utilities; in others, you must hire plumbers, electricians, etc.)

INSPECTING YOUR HOME

❏ Have you checked over the home, both inside and out, to see if everything is in order and working properly?

❏ Do all doors, windows, and drawers close properly? Binding doors, etc., may signal that the home is not properly leveled.

❏ Do all appliances and faucets work?

❏ Did you make a list of all problems when you moved in, and did you report the problems to the dealer and to the manufacturer?

11
Reviewing Options: Modular, Panelized, and Pre-Cut Homes

MODULAR AND PANELIZED HOMES

As we noted in Chapter 9, costs associated with the building site are pretty well locked in, regardless of the type of housing to be placed on the site, so there is often little or no cost savings possible when choosing between the conventional site-built house and modular or panelized housing. Also, both modular housing and panelized housing require site set-up or assembly by professional erection crews, so usually no do-it-yourself savings are possible through labor or sweat equity. Why then would a buyer choose either modular or panelized housing over conventional housing?

Modular and panelized housing, though they may in many cases be comparable in price to stick-built houses and thus may offer little dollar savings, still can offer some advantages over stick-built homes, and continue to be an optional choice for many home buyers, for a variety of reasons.

Economies Possible with Factory-Built Housing

The question of costs for building materials is dependent on a number of factors. First, a high-volume factory that assembles many homes may have a significant advantage in buying power over a small local builder. As with most products, buying building materials in large quantity — truckload or even train carload lots — may result in significant

savings. But stick-built housing contractors who build large projects may be able to buy building materials in large quantities and thus buy them as cheaply as builders of modular housing. However, many companies that specialize in modular or panelized housing insist that their superior buying power means they can buy the best building materials at the lowest prices, and therefore can offer a better finished product than the small stick-builder.

Weather-Controlled Construction

Another advantage of modular or panelized housing over stick-building is that with factory-built housing one can have weather-controlled construction. One of the significant drawbacks to stick-built housing is that the building materials are subjected to damage or problems from extremes in humidity or temperature during construction. I well remember, for example, a house that was framed in the fall of the year. It rained almost daily that fall, and the carpenters took advantage of any short break in the weather to continue framing progress. Framing lumber that was "kiln dried" when purchased became saturated with moisture, and swelled accordingly. On the first sunny day, after the framing was well saturated, the carpenters applied the plywood sheathing and thus blocked any chance that air could move through the structure and dry out the framing.

I remember the house well because I was then a drywall contractor. After the house was closed in, or sheathed, the owner asked for two bids: one from me, for a drywall or wallboard interior, the other from one of the best plastering contractors in the business. After some deliberation, the owner awarded the plastering contractor the job. Rather than being disappointed, I breathed a sigh of relief. I knew that when that lumber shrank, the plaster contractor was going to have nothing but complaints from the owner, as framing shrank and plaster cracked. That proved to be the case: the owner forever complained that the plasterers had done a "poor job." Of course, had the house been allowed to stand for a while so the framing lumber could dry out before the interior plaster work was done, this problem could have been avoided. But everyone is in a hurry, and buy now, pay later is a common mistake in home building. This type of problem is avoided when housing is factory-built, because the components are assembled under roof, with temperature and humidity controlled.

Painting Problems

Another job that suffers from on-site application is painting, both interior and exterior. One often-neglected truth about painting is that the quality of any paint job depends on a controlled drying rate for the paint. For example, if ceilings are spray-textured in a site-built house, while temperatures are cold and humidity is high (in the spring or fall), the texture paint will dry too slowly. This slow drying can result in rust spots over nails or screwheads, when moisture lingers over the steel fastener. Slow paint drying also can cause discolored streaks in the wallboard, over the joints, or can cause moisture to soak into the treated joints and make them become swollen and distorted. This condition in drywall or wallboard construction is known as *joint beading* or *ridging*.

Vandalism and Theft

Another possible advantage of factory-built housing is the reduction of vandalism when compared to site-built housing. Adventuresome children are at-tracted to building sites. I have seen houses where vandals opened gallons of paint, roofing tar, or adhesives and splattered them over the house's interior. This not only wastes the paint or other material, it also damages or destroys the materials upon which the paint is splattered. In one case, I remember the paint was dumped over hundreds of dollars worth of oak strip flooring, and the flooring was totally beyond reclaiming when the vandalism was discovered the following morning.

There is also the possibility of injury to curious children when site-built homes are erected. In one disastrous case, small children piled up concrete blocks and climbed up on the blocks to look into a barrel of slaking plaster. Slaking plaster can become extremely hot, as a result of the chemical action of the lime. A child fell into the plaster barrel and was badly burned. Her parents sued the builder for damages and won. Another example of potential job site hazards is the danger of injuries when trespassing children climb ladders or scaffolding that is left in place overnight. Dangerous or even fatal falls can result, and the builder of the house is legally liable for maintaining an "attractive nuisance"; i.e., a condition that may attract and be a hazard to neighborhood children. By contrast, modular or panelized houses can be secured from vandals or other intruders more quickly than site-built houses. Often, the factory-built houses can be locked after just one day's assembly time.

Theft of building materials can also be better controlled with panelized or modular housing than with site-built homes. On a Friday afternoon at one housing project, I watched the lumber yard deliver banded pallets of framing lumber, enough lumber to build a three-bedroom house. When the building crew showed up on Monday morning, not one 2 x 4 was left on the site. Who stole the lumber? We never found the culprit. Smaller but expensive components, such as windows, furnaces, or water heaters are easily picked up and hauled away, leaving the owner or builder to foot the costs. Modular houses, with components already assembled, are not such an inviting target for thieves.

Time is Money

Yet another advantage of modular or panelized housing is the speed of erection and early possible occupancy. Site-built houses regularly require a building schedule of ninety days or more; custom-built houses often require even more time, sometimes as much as one year to complete. Time is money. Someone — ultimately, the buyer — must pay the interest charge for the time the house building is in progress but not occupied during construction. Not only does factory construction eliminate the adverse effects of weather on the building materials, it also eliminates the construction time delays that can slow down or halt progress on site-built houses, when weather becomes too cold or too wet for work to progress. This reduction in erection time means there is a corresponding reduction in the cost of interest for a "bridge loan" or interim financing.

Cost Overruns

Another consideration that can affect a house-buying decision is the possibility of cost overruns. Having a firm dollar cost in advance is particularly important when government agencies are purchasing the housing for low-income, elderly, or other subsidized housing. Panelized or modular housing is available at a fixed price, a price that is not affected by delays, labor overruns, or other cost variables that can drive up final costs on stick-built housing. It is easier to work with a firm bid than to be faced with the unhappy prospect of a "surprise" in the form of thousands of dollars in cost overruns when a building is completed.

Lower Labor Costs

Factory-built housing may also be assembled or built with lower-cost labor than is possible for stick-built housing. Much of the labor of building a house on site may be done by highly skilled, and also highly paid, union tradesmen, but housing factories may employ workers at lower hourly rates. Many of the jobs that require skilled labor when done on site are, in the factory, divided up into small, repetitive tasks that can easily be performed by workers who have only a minimum of skills and training. This may let the housing manufacturer pass along some savings in labor costs to the buyer.

One other consideration relative to the cost of labor is the general availability of skilled labor. During the years of the last housing boom, construction tradesmen were in short supply in many major housing markets. The residential construction labor force was, until recently, made up of those who learned their construction trades in the Navy Seabees or other branches of the service, during World War II. Younger workers went into the trades during the booming postwar decades of the 1960s and 1970s. But the inflationary years of the latter 1970s and early 1980s made the residential construction business a roller coaster of good and bad years. Younger workers were discouraged from going into the building trades at the same time the old-timers were aging toward their retirement years and phasing out of the labor force. As a result, there was a labor shortage in the construction industries during recent boom years, and many buyers, including government agencies that were buying subsidized housing, turned to factory-built housing as an available alternative.

PRE-CUT HOUSING

Generally speaking, pre-cut housing is not considered to be "manufactured housing" because the only work done for the buyer is the mathematics and labor of cutting the various components for size and angle. Pre-cut housing kits usually are available with all the framing members already cut to fit: roof trusses are already assembled. For the novice, this cut-to-fit material removes the guesswork of measuring and cutting, avoiding wasted time and ruined or miscut materials. These pre-cut home kits can then be bought by the consumer unassembled, or can be purchased in various stages of completion. For example, the buyer might have the basement or foundation built, and choose to assemble the house from scratch using his own and volunteer labor — known as "sweat equity." Options include having the housing company frame and "close in" the house, leaving only exterior siding, roofing, and interior finishing for the owner either to do himself or to hire local contractors to do the work. Or the buyer can buy the kit house and have all the construction site work done by the company that supplies the kit, doing little or none of the assembly work himself.

Determining Savings

What savings are possible if you choose a pre-cut kit house, doing all or some of the construction yourself? The savings are difficult to compute, because the amount saved varies widely by geographical region, by housing density (urban vs. suburban vs. small town vs. rural), by local labor costs, and by the cost of building permits and other governmental charges. If you had thought that government costs were insignificant, consider that building permit costs in Chapter 12 show that permit costs can be as low as $114.00 in Las Cruces, New Mexico, or as high as $10,000.00 in Ft. Collins, Colorado. The total cost of government taxing and regulation of new housing may add as much as 20 percent to the final cost of the house.

Savings possible with "sweat equity" depend on how much and in what fields you are willing to sweat. For example, painting is one chore often left to the owner; but painting accounts for only a small portion of the cost of a house, so you cannot save many dollars if your sweat equity is limited to doing your own painting. You must do more, or other, phases of the house construction to realize large savings on your own labor.

In Chapter 12, we explore further the discussion of whether you should attempt to save housing dollars by doing all or some of the contracting or labor yourself. Keep in mind that building a house is a major undertaking, one that should not be entered into lightly. Can you build your own house? Certainly; thousands have done so. But you should be aware of the potential rewards, as well as the potential hazards, before making the final decision. If you do decide to build your own house, a reference such as *The Complete Guide to Contracting Your Home*, 2nd edition, may prove very helpful.

MODULAR/PANELIZED HOUSING: COMPANY PROFILES

Transporting entire houses about is an expensive proposition, and the costs of transporting them may make marketing manufactured homes on a national scale cost-prohibitive. Many firms that are engaged in the factory-built housing business are regional in nature, selling houses only within a radius of a few hundred miles of their factories. However, if you live in any sizable city, you will be able to find a builder/dealer of manufactured homes in the phone book Yellow Pages.

Following are profiles of two companies that sell manufactured housing. I chose these two companies as examples because I have a nodding acquaintanceship with both companies. A friend of mine became a dealer for Wausau Homes in the early 1960s, when Wausau was a fledgling company. I worked with Miles Lumber, later to become Miles Homes, on a number of their homes through the 1950s and '60s. Both companies are located in the upper Midwest: Wausau Homes is based in Wausau, Wisconsin, and Miles Homes offices are in suburban Minneapolis, Minnesota.

Wausau Homes

Stick builders are at their most efficient when building in large tracts, where economy can be achieved by virtue of quantity buying of materials and cookie-cutter repetition of housing units. Manufactured or panelized houses become competitive in price when they are used as a single-project effort on scattered building lots, where there is no repetition of effort. In 1975, *Automated Builder* magazine called Wausau Homes "the Midwest's paragon of scattered lot builders." In the roller-coaster housing market of the 1970s, Wausau Homes produced a high total of more than 4,000 houses. In a fading housing market of 1989, annual unit production still held above the 3,000 mark.

Wausau Homes began as a local sawmill, back in the Depression decade of the 1930s. By 1960, Wausau was producing electronically-bonded (heat-activated adhesives), closed-wall house panels in a

16,000 square foot plant. The company built a total of fifteen such houses in that first year.

Today, more than thirty years later, Wausau Homes has produced more than 90,000 housing units and grosses more than $80 million in housing sales over a ten-state marketing area. The company occupies a 300,000 square foot plant on a seventy-seven-acre complex. Wausau Homes today includes the parent company, Wausau Homes, producing open panel units, closed panel units, mechanical cores and modulars (wall/floor units that contain plumbing and wiring, for kitchen and bathroom areas); Wausau Homes branch plants in Gray, Georgia and in Lake Wales, Florida, which produce modular homes; Sterling Building Systems, purchased in the late 1970s to produce open-panel custom homes; and Advance Building Systems, which produces open panel units in Paulding, Ohio and in Charleston, Illinois.

In the June 1990 issue, *Automated Builder* magazine ranked Wausau Homes as the third largest panelized home producer in the U.S. However, Wausau Homes points out that the companies that were ranked as #1 (Ryland Homes) and #2 (NVR Building Products) are primarily production builders, producing houses in their own plants for their own accounts, while Wausau Homes sells homes through four hundred builder/dealers and thus by traditional definition should be ranked as #1.

Rather than using cheap building materials to achieve cost competitiveness, Wausau Homes uses name brand quality building materials and their sizable buying power as the means of offering a quality product while holding costs down. Wausau consumes trainloads of building materials each year. Brand names you may recognize include Armstrong vinyl flooring; Mansfield, Moen, and Kohler plumbing equipment; Weyerhaeuser and Louisiana-Pacific building products; Certainteed roofing shingles and vinyl siding (other siding options are available); GE electrical products and Thomas lighting; Merillat cabinets; Owens-Corning Fiberglass insulation; Paslode fasteners; Norco Windows; Peachtree doors; and Schlage locks.

In order to market homes in ten states, as Wausau Homes does, the units must be built to meet the most stringent state and national building and energy codes. The home buyer is thus guaranteed of getting a product that is built to exacting standards. A completely computerized operation lets the customer benefit from: Computer-Aided Drafting (CAD) for faster turn-around of plans and drawings; Computer-Integrated Building (CIB), which generates graphics for factory-built components and for on-site assembly construction; plus computerized truss design and ordering/processing of the contract and all related paperwork.

Careful handling in delivery of the units is achieved because Wausau Homes also owns WH Transportation. WH Transportation began when Wausau Homes started a semi-truck fleet to deliver their home packages. Today, WH Transportation is engaged in home delivery, plus doing business as a common carrier. In addition to the truck fleet, WH Transportation has truck-mounted cranes that hoist the heavy panels and modules into position for assembly at the job site.

On-site assembly of the Wausau home panels and modules is done by experienced building crews, at the direction of local builder/dealers. Because the panels are large and heavy, house assembly is not a do-it-yourself project. There is no possibility of saving via "sweat equity" with most panelized houses. But other advantages over stick building remain. The panelized house buyer knows the exact final cost of the unit, so there are no unhappy surprises; construction of the panels is done in a factory under climate-controlled conditions; job-site vandalism and theft are reduced or eliminated; there are no building-in-progress fees or interest charges; and the house is quickly completed and ready for occupancy in the time it takes a stick-builder to unload his tools.

If you would like to explore the Wausau Homes approach, contact:

Wausau Homes Inc.
P.O. Box 8005
Wausau, WI 54402-8005
(715) 359-7272

Buying materials in carload quantities yields significant savings on building materials. Courtesy of Wausau Homes, Inc.

Forklifts move pallets of framing lumber to proper work station for assembly. Courtesy of Wausau Homes, Inc.

Floor panels incorporate floor joists and subfloor plywood. Workers apply panel adhesive for strong, squeak-free floor. Courtesy of Wausau Homes, Inc.

Roof trusses are designed on a computer, assembled on the plant assembly line. Courtesy of Wausau Homes, Inc.

Wall panels may be closed, incorporate exterior sheathing, insulation, doors, and windows. Courtesy of Wausau Homes, Inc.

Assembly worker installs electrical outlets in wall panel. Courtesy of Wausau Homes, Inc.

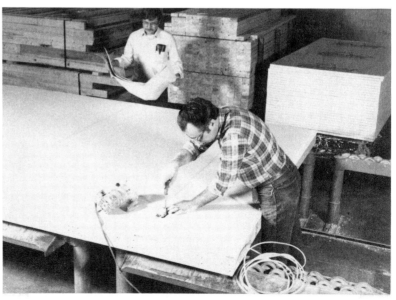

Modular units such as this bathroom core are shipped as completely finished rooms, with all plumbing, wiring, and fixtures installed. Courtesy of Wausau Homes, Inc.

Millwork such as interior doors is prepared for assembly, with hinges mortised and lock holes bored. Courtesy of Wausau Homes, Inc.

Wausau truck arrives at the job site with modular and panelized units ready for assembly. Courtesy of Wausau Homes, Inc.

Large panels and modular units are unloaded and lifted into place by large cranes. Courtesy of Wausau Homes, Inc.

The center support beam is hoisted into position atop the basement foundation. Courtesy of Wausau Homes, Inc.

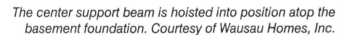

The floor panels are hoisted from the flatbed trailer via the crane, and positioned atop the foundation wall and center beam. Courtesy of Wausau Homes, Inc.

Workers position the floor panels, check for square, and secure the panels in place. Courtesy of Wausau Homes, Inc.

As the crane operator gently lowers the panel atop the walls, workers guide the second-story floor panel into position. Courtesy of Wausau Homes, Inc.

The crane operator lowers a wall panel into position while a worker guides the panel so the panels meet squarely at the corner. Courtesy of Wausau Homes, Inc.

With the second-story floor panels in place, the walls to the second story are raised via the crane. Courtesy of Wausau Homes, Inc.

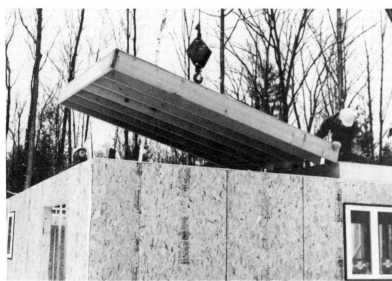

View from the underside shows the strength and rigidity of the floor panels. Panel adhesive assembly helps to strengthen the final floor. Courtesy of Wausau Homes, Inc.

Floor dimensions are checked, and panel alignment is carefully monitored by the worker. Courtesy of Wausau Homes, Inc.

All in a day's work: the house walls are erected, roof trusses in place, in just one work day.
Courtesy of Wausau Homes, Inc.

The finished house shown is the corporate "Feature Home," model C-405. The 1½ story home
contains 2,280 square feet of floor space on both floors. Courtesy of Wausau Homes, Inc.

Miles Homes

Can the average non-professional person build his or her own home? Miles Homes, Inc. will bet that, within reason, he can. And Miles Homes has more than 35,000 successful case histories/customers to prove their point.

We must note that back in the exciting days of the 1950s housing booms, blue-suede shoe salesmen oversold the do-it-yourself possibilities of pre-cut or panelized homes. Many young couples, with absolutely no building experience or knowledge, were convinced that building a house of their own was as easy and enjoyable as a day at the beach. Many of these early victims got into trouble, as work took longer than expected, certain projects proved beyond the abilities of the couple to perform, and the months dragged on with no project completion date in sight. Miles Homes was one of the first companies to recognize that it was in their own best interests to screen prospective customers more carefully, and to provide a greater degree of help or "hand-holding" of the customer throughout the house-building project. It is not in the best interests of either the company or the customer to get people into projects they cannot expect to complete.

Miles Homes began their effort to help the consumer build homes way back in 1946, so they speak with some experience and authority. But Miles Homes has adopted a unique approach to the do-it-yourself movement; an approach that includes screening, consultation, education, and financing to ensure that their house-building "partners" have a good chance of finishing what they begin. To guarantee this effort, Miles Homes has a backup staff that is as near as the customer's telephone. At any step, the customer can call Miles people who will "bail you out" of any corner the customer may have gotten himself into. And a key to the success of the Miles Homes Owner Builder Program is that Miles will supply interim financing while the house is being built, and assist the customer in converting the bridge or interim loan into a conventional mortgage when the house is finished.

How can you begin on the road to building your own Miles home? The first step is to contact Miles Homes at 1-800-343-2884. Miles representatives will direct you to one of their informational home-building seminars, which are held in most areas of the country.

At the seminar, you will meet with a local Miles New Home Consultant. The consultant will guide you through the steps you will have to take to embark on the Owner Builder Program. Through this program Miles claims to work with the buyer through the planning and blueprint stages, into construction and financing. They supply you with quality materials to build the house and provide you with do-it-yourself instructional manuals and videotapes. This process Miles calls "one source convenience," and states that "building it yourself never means building it alone."

When you get to the actual construction phase, you alone decide how much of the actual building you will do, building all or any part of the house yourself. You can subcontract to others any portion of the work that you don't feel comfortable doing yourself.

Construction financing is provided at below-market interest rates. Your monthly loan payment is for interest only while you build. When the house is completed, you choose a lender (with Miles' help and direction) and use the mortgage money to repay the Miles construction loan.

Miles Financing Plan Summary

Here, slightly paraphrased, is a summary of the Miles Homes, Inc. Financing Plan:

❏ Check local building codes before starting to build. In some areas, restrictions dictate that some portions of the job must be performed by licensed tradespersons. In most instances, these restrictions against doing it yourself concern the mechanical trades of plumbing, heating, and electrical work. Also, your own personal building experience may dictate that you need some help with masonry, finish carpentry, or other skilled chores.

❏ To secure their own mortgage interests, Miles Homes decrees that the buyer/builder must offer them a recordable Mortgage or Deed of Trust for the real estate (building lot) upon which you will build your house. This provides Miles with a security interest so that they can advance construction monies to you. Miles may further require that you supply them with a copy of the land contract or a bill of sale for the land.

❏ If your property is already mortgaged and you cannot supply Miles Homes with a first mortgage, Miles will seek satisfactory agreements with mortgagees who have prior financial interest in the property. This is done before any building materials are shipped.

❏ Plan carefully: you will be charged for extras accordingly, to the extent that such extras are not included in the original purchase price.

❏ The house price quoted by Miles will include two deliveries: one for framing materials, another delivery for finish materials. Any extra deliveries for unplanned materials will be charged to the customer.

❏ All material shipments should be sorted and inventoried as soon as they are unloaded, to be sure that all materials shipped are accounted for.

❏ The customer will have available a series of prescribed steps to follow in the event of any disagreements. If you cannot get satisfaction within a preset time, there is a "Homeowner's Hotline Memo" you can send to Miles Homes Vice President of Consumer Affairs. He will either provide satisfaction on the complaint or will forward your memo for review by a corporate officer who will contact you promptly. No fee is charged for this prompt review and resolution of customer complaints.

❏ A complete Specifications Sheet, listing all the components in the Miles Homes package, will be provided to you by your Miles Homes representative.

❏ Monthly payments during the construction period are for interest only, and will not reduce the amount of your construction loan owed to Miles Homes.

Like Wausau Homes, Miles Homes stresses the use of quality building materials, noting there is a great difference between buying a cheap house and buying a house cheap. Major brand-name building products supplied include Owens-Corning Fiberglass, American Standard plumbing fixtures, Delta faucets, GAF Roofing, Riviera Kitchens, Weather Shield Wood Windows, and Masonite Siding.

For more information on Miles Homes, Inc., contact:

Miles Homes, Inc.
4700 Nathan Lane
P.O. Box 9495
Minneapolis, MN 55440
(800) 343-2884

Worker checks blueprints for accuracy in Miles panel plant. Courtesy of Miles Homes.

Miles Homes employs computer design and sophisticated tools to control production costs.
Courtesy of Miles Homes.

Building materials are prepared and delivered to the job site in two shipments: first, the framing package (shown) and later the finish materials. Courtesy of Miles Homes.

When the material delivery is unloaded, make a careful inventory to be sure you have received all the materials listed on the bill of lading. Courtesy of Miles Homes.

One of the more difficult jobs, and one you may wish to have a professional do, is laying the basement or foundation walls. Courtesy of Miles Homes.

After the floor joists are set, subfloor plywood is nailed on to form the house floor or deck. Courtesy of Miles Homes.

The panelized stud walls are numbered to guide proper assembly. Panels reduce on-site measuring and cutting work. Courtesy of Miles Homes.

After raising the exterior wall panels, install the interior stud walls. All stud wall panels are numbered for easy assembly. Courtesy of Miles Homes.

When stud wall panels and roof trusses are assembled, the next step is to install roof and wall sheathing. Courtesy of Miles Homes.

The house is shown fully sheathed, ready for roofing and siding application. Roof sheathing is plywood; wall sheathing is Owens-Corning Energy Shield foam panels for better insulation. Courtesy of Miles Homes.

Energy Shield wall sheathing has a foil face that resists penetration by air or moisture. Courtesy of Miles Homes.

Masonite siding is nailed over the sidewall sheathing to complete the exterior work. Courtesy of Miles Homes.

Owner/builder uses a cordless screwdriver to attach upper cabinets to the kitchen wall. Courtesy of Miles Homes.

Finished kitchen with appliances installed, ready to go to work. Courtesy of Miles Homes.

Exterior of the house is nearing completion, ready to button up and landscape.
Courtesy of Miles Homes.

Final lot work includes grading, sodding, planting trees and shrubs. Plan carefully: if well
executed, landscaping can greatly increase the value of your home. Courtesy of Miles Homes.

Houses are available in many sizes and styles, such as the two-story shown here. Any given plan can be altered to suit your own needs. Courtesy of Miles Homes.

A split entry home lets you utilize lower level more fully. A major key to success: all those helpful hands. Courtesy of Miles Homes.

This model, called the Grandview, is available in three optional floor plans. The L-shaped porch helps make this one of Miles' more popular models. Courtesy of Miles Homes.

The two-story South Hampton model can be either three or four bedrooms, in 1,653 square feet to 2,244 square feet of floor space. Miles offers fifty different home designs. Courtesy of Miles Homes.

12
Sweat Equity: Should You Do It Yourself?

I have spent half a lifetime telling people how to do their own home remodeling and repair. But it is a long stretch from doing your own small projects to building an entire house. First, let us recognize that many thousands of people, even people who began building as complete amateurs with absolutely no building experience, have built their own houses. At the same time, many thousands of people who have tried being their own contractor or builder have gotten in far over their heads, and have ended up in very unhappy situations.

BUILDING YOUR OWN HOME IS NOT FOR JUST ANYONE

Once, over-eager kit home salesmen were inclined to talk the unwary into buying and building their kit house. Eventually, companies that sold pre-cut homes realized that it was not in their best interest to become involved with do-it-yourselfer customers who were "all thumbs" and who were not likely to be able to complete a home building project successfully. Today, reputable kit or panel home companies attempt to weed out the "unhandy" and to sell house kits to those who have the abilities necessary to complete their projects successfully.

Regardless of what building magazine editors may advise, building a house is a very large and complicated undertaking, even for an experienced person. In the days when all houses were stick-built, the industry estimated that the average house represented a full year's work (2,000 person-hours) for one person. In today's building climate, when components such as roof trusses, pre-finished cabinets, and pre-hung doors may reduce the amount of on-site labor required to build a house, building a house still is not a "part-time" undertaking for the average person. It requires much time, effort, skill, and perseverance to build a house. You should think the situation over very carefully before committing to building your own house. Here are some of the things you should consider before deciding to build your own home, or to serve as your own contractor.

TIME

When deciding whether to be your own contractor/ builder, the first thing to consider is your own time schedule. Depending on the size of the house you will build, you can easily spend up to 2,000 person-hours building a house. That 2,000 hours represents fifty forty-hour weeks, or a full work year for the average worker. So, if you put in your regular work week at a salaried job, then put in another full forty-hour work week working nights and weekends on a house, you will be working 16-hour days — more, if you consider travel time to and from the building site — for at least a year to complete your house. Sound enticing? That sort of schedule is for the very able-bodied and ambitious.

And you are sure to have building-related interruptions at your job during your regular work day. Can you take personal calls at your workplace, to make buying choices or planning decisions? Does your schedule permit you to come in late in the morning, or to take long lunch hours, to consult with tradesmen or suppliers? If your job situation will not permit you to be away during part of the work day, you may not be a candidate for contracting your own house.

HEALTH

You must be in rigorous good health to put in double work weeks, and the long days alone can be a drag. But building is also physically taxing work. One contractor we know complained that "everything I pick up weighs more than I do." Building consists of lifting, hauling, and climbing, and you must be able-bodied to perform the work.

HANDYMAN SKILLS

Are you handy and experienced with both power and hand tools? All construction tools are designed to cut, carve, and/or abrade any surface with which they come in contact, including your skin. If you are not comfortable using tools, you may expose yourself to potentially serious injury on a construction job. Consider carefully your own skill levels before deciding to build a house yourself.

How do you feel about climbing and working on ladders or on other high platforms? Many people simply are afraid of heights. Setting roof rafters or trusses, or installing roof sheathing, shingles, or flashing, requires that you be comfortable while working at heights. The only option is to have friends in high places who will help or will do some or all of the scaffold work for you.

HELPERS

Many building components are heavy and/or large and awkward to handle, thus requiring two people for installation. Windows, pre-hung doors, plywood sheathing, floor joists, and roof rafters or trusses all require two people for handling. If you have family or friends who are willing to help when needed, you have overcome one large obstacle to

being your own builder. Keep in mind, however, that when all is said and done, there is more said than done. Those promises of endless help from friends and relatives, given so enthusiastically when the house project is a plan on a kitchen table, tend to fade away when it comes time to get to the actual hard work and long hours required to build a house. Super Bowl games, the opening of the hunting and fishing seasons, or hot/cold/rainy days will tend to have a diminishing and negative effect on the enthusiasm of your volunteer work force. You can count on it.

Consider also not only the quantity but the quality of the labor offered. The helpful klutz who always forgets to bring his hammer to the job site is not going to be much help, no matter how sincere his intentions. The uncle who is a licensed plumber, the brother who has his electrician's license, or the father-in-law who is a mason are the people who can really contribute significant and valuable efforts to your building project. Lacking really experienced help, you should seriously consider paying a contractor to do the job. Work overtime at your own job, or take an extra part-time job to earn extra money, rather than trying to make money at construction jobs for which you are neither trained nor equipped.

TOOLS

Having the right tools for any given project is a critical requisite for doing a workmanlike job. But keep in mind that tools are expensive, and often it does not pay to make the tool investment for doing a job yourself. To equip yourself for building a house, you can easily invest hundreds or thousands of dollars in assorted hand and power tools. If you must buy expensive stationary power tools, such as a table saw or radial arm saw, tools you may not use again after the house is done, the projected tool investment alone may be a critical factor in your decision as to whether to build your own house.

Do not ignore or underestimate the size of this tool investment: anyone who has tried building his own house will tell you that tool purchases can be an expensive and weekly drain on the building budget, as each week brings a new building project for which you must buy more special tools. Be sure to add a few hundred dollars to your projected tool budget, just to handle those unforeseen tool purchases.

ESTIMATING DO-IT-YOURSELFER SAVINGS

Before deciding to act as your own contractor or to build all or part of your own house, try to estimate your projected savings. Editors of housing books and magazines sometimes overstate the possible savings from doing your own work, making the work seem more valuable financially than it really is. The result may be that consumers undertake a project on the basis of inflated savings expectations, and may then be very frustrated when the project has been completed with great personal effort but the promised dollar savings do not materialize. We will help you to estimate more closely the savings possible by doing a given project yourself, so you can make a realistic estimate. Knowing the real dollar savings range for a project that you are considering may convince you that the effort necessary to perform the task is not worth the small financial return that may result.

Geographic Differences
Be aware that the cost of labor, and to a lesser degree the cost of materials, may vary widely between large urban areas and small towns or rural areas. The labor costs will also vary widely between geographic regions. Labor costs more in the large cities of the north and east, where workers are organized into labor unions, than in the right-to-work or non-union areas of the west and south. You will find that the cost per square foot of hiring a contractor to build a house, including all materials and labor, can vary from a high of $107.06 per square foot in New Haven-Meriden Connecticut, down to $22.93 per square foot in Austin, Texas. Obviously, the cheaper cost per square foot in Austin, Texas might convince you that doing the work yourself might prove less than amply reward-

ing. You might be more tempted to build your own house in New York, New York, where cost-per-square-foot is $68.43, than in Phoenix, Arizona, where having a house built by pros costs $28.13 per square foot. (All quoted figures are from the Economics Department of the National Association of Home Builders.)

Following is a list of sixty-six major cities from the National Association of Home Builders (NAHB) that compares the cost per square foot for professional builders to build a house in various metropolitan areas. The list is not complete, but you should be able to find a dollar figure from a city similar in size to your own, in the same geographical area, and compare it to your own locale to arrive at a workable cost estimate.

DO-IT-YOURSELF SAVINGS BY JOB

Following are example charts showing total building costs broken down by project. The charts are from the National Association of Home Builders, "Construction Costs By Metro Area" (September 1990), and show costs-by-job for randomly selected cities. As noted earlier, it is very difficult to make any blanket cost assumptions that would apply to the entire country. But we surveyed the entire list of sixty-six cities and reached the following conclusions.

Painting
Doing your own exterior painting may save varying amounts of money, depending on the location and the size of the house. But for the average-size house, in most cities across the nation, the cost for exterior house painting will be no more than $1,200.00 to $1,500.00, including the cost of the paint and tools. Obviously, doing your own exterior painting cannot save you vast amounts of money, when the labor cost for painting the average house might be only $1,000.00 total.

As you will see in the charts, interior painting will cost (labor and materials) between three percent and five percent of the total cost of the house, so that is the potential savings range for doing your own

CONSTRUCTION COSTS BY METRO AREA

Metro Area	Cost per Square Foot
Amarillo, TX	$32.10
Anaheim-Santa Ana, CA	$40.81
Anchorage, AK	$44.39
Atlanta, GA	$34.76
Aurora-Elgin, IL	$51.08
Austin, TX	$22.93
Baltimore, MD	$41.11
Bergen-Passaic, NJ	$44.23
Birmingham, AL	$32.54
Boston, MA	$47.74
Canton, OH	$31.61
Charleston, SC	$33.34
Charlotte-Gastonia-Rock Hill, NC/SC	$39.70
Chicago, IL	$35.52
Cincinnati, OH/KY/IN	$32.46
Cleveland, OH	$45.88
Colorado Springs, CO	$30.67
Columbus, OH	$41.29
Dallas, TX	$32.03
Daytona Beach, FL	$32.21
Denver, CO	$31.66
Detroit, MI	$42.74
Ft. Collins-Loveland, CO	$41.67
Ft. Lauderdale-Hollywood, FL	$36.25
Ft. Worth-Arlington, TX	$49.18
Fresno, CA	$32.29
Gary-Hammond, IN	$36.50
Grand Rapids, MI	$30.28
Greensboro-Winston-Salem-High Point, NC	$31.57
Houston, TX	$29.22
Indianapolis, IN	$36.49
La Crosse, WI	$42.36
Lake County, IL	$47.34

Metro Area	Cost per Square Foot
Lafayette, IN	$40.38
Las Cruces, NM	$32.70
Las Vegas, NV	$33.57
Lewiston-Auburn, ME	$61.79
Los Angeles-Long Beach, CA	$69.24
Memphis, TN/AR/MS	$45.96
Minneapolis-St. Paul, MN/WI	$43.95
Muskegon, MI	$45.71
Nashville, TN	$39.87
Nassau-Suffolk, NY	$48.96
New Haven-Meriden, CT	$107.06
New York, NY	$68.43
Norfolk-Virginia Beach-Newport News, VA	$34.18
Oakland, CA	$40.34
Oklahoma City, OK	$33.96
Orlando, FL	$62.11
Philadelphia, PA	$36.07
Phoenix, AZ	$28.13
Raleigh-Durham, NC	$53.47
Richmond-Petersburg, VA	$37.09
Riverside-San Bernardino, CA	$34.77
Sacramento, CA	$45.11
St. Louis, MO/IL	$55.36
San Diego, CA	$40.11
San Francisco, CA	$51.37
Seattle, WA	$37.77
Sioux Falls, SD	$27.25
Tallahassee, FL	$38.64
Tampa-St. Petersburg-Clearwater, FL	$32.07
Toledo, OH	$54.35
Tulsa, OK	$27.38
Washington, DC/MD/VA	$42.69
West Palm Beach, FL	$54.35

The above list is courtesy of the Economics Department, National Association of Home Builders, "Construction Costs By Metro Area," September 1990.

interior painting. Look carefully at the true dollar total that the builder will allow for interior painting, and try to estimate closely what portion of that total will be spent for paint and tools. Again, is what you may save worth the hassle of meeting construction deadlines?

Drywall

Another area that may be suggested for do-it-yourselfers is the drywall or wallboard work. Here again, a study of all the cities in the NAHB survey reveals that the dollar savings for doing your own drywall work may vary between 2.9 percent of the total house cost in New Haven, Connecticut, up to 6.2 percent of the total cost in Norfolk, Virginia. But in most cities the drywall work, including materials, will range between three and four percent of the total cost of the house. This would be in return for installing (hanging) and finishing around 5,000 square feet of wallboard, or just over a hundred 4' x 12' panels. As a former drywall contractor, I can tell you that, for the amateur, this is a tough way to save a buck.

Interior Trim

Doing the interior trim for a house requires considerable skill, for a return that will average somewhere between two percent and three percent of the total cost of the house. This will vary widely because generally there is much less wood trim used today than was once true. For example, in many areas, the drywall contractor now finishes closet door openings with metal corner bead, rather than the carpenter having to install wood jambs and casing as once was true.

Building Permits

One eye-opener for many of us may be the wide variation between cities in the cost of building permits. For example, paying for building permits may cost a low of $114.00 in Las Cruces, New Mexico, up to a high of $10,000.00 in Ft. Collins-Loveland, Colorado. A study of the government costs for building permits reveals that in major cities the government can have a significant impact on housing costs via elevated costs for building permits and through unfair or exclusionary zoning requirements.

Following are charts that review construction costs by project for eight metropolitan areas. The examples I chose include Minneapolis/St. Paul, Minnesota (my home); Denver, Colorado; Tulsa, Oklahoma; St. Louis, Missouri; Phoenix, Arizona, and West Palm Beach, Florida. These charts reveal housing examples that might reasonably be considered as "affordable" housing. Atypical examples chosen include New York, New York and San Diego, California, where the housing examples show cost breakdowns for projects on houses in the $300,000.00 price range. By matching your own city against a city shown, one of comparable size and geographic location, you may be able to estimate the project cost range for your area, and to gauge your own possible do-it-yourself savings.

METRO AREA: DENVER, CO

Finished Area (sq. ft.):	1,370
Size of Lot (sq. ft.):	4,600

SALES PRICE BREAKDOWN

Total Construction Cost:	$51,750.00
Finished Lot Cost:	16,250.00
Total Financing Costs:	900.00
Land Acquisition and Development Financing:	220.00
Construction Financing:	680.00
Profit, Overhead, and General Operating Expenses:	24,920.00
Total Sales Price:	$93,820.00

Denver, CO

	Average	Percent of Total
Building Permits	$1,465.00	3.4%
Architectural	-.-	-.-
Excavation/Backfill	400.00	0.9%
Footings/Foundation	3,804.00	8.8%
Waterproofing	55.00	0.1%
Termite Protection	-.-	-.-
Concrete Flatwork	2,255.00	5.2%
Framing for Decks/Walls	11,595.00	26.7%
Framing for Roof	-.-	-.-
Roofing	990.00	2.3%
Gutters/Downspouts	320.00	0.7%
Windows/Skylights	1,000.00	2.3%
Exterior Doors	290.00	0.7%
Insulation	764.00	1.8%
Siding/Exterior Trim	-.-	-.-
HVAC	1,206.00	2.8%
Drywall	2,421.00	5.6%
Interior Painting	507.00	1.2%
Ceramic Tile Walls & Floors	1,106.00	2.6%
Carpet	-.-	-.-
Wood Flooring	-.-	-.-
Vinyl Flooring	-.-	-.-
Other Flooring	-.-	-.-
Interior Trim Carpentry	-.-	-.-
Interior Doors	-.-	-.-
Ceramic Tile Countertop	-.-	-.-
Cabinets/Vanities	1,050.00	2.4%
Appliances	560.00	1.3%
Rough and Finish Plumbing	2,485.00	5.7%
Rough and Finish Electrical	1,348.00	3.1%
Lighting Fixtures	217.00	0.5%
Exterior Painting	507.00	1.2%

Landscaping	650.00	1.5%
Driveway	-.-	-.-
Exterior Structures	-.-	-.-
Final Cleanup	75.00	0.2%
Fireplace	400.00	0.9%
Swimming Pool	-.-	-.-
Greenhouse	-.-	-.-
Other	6,900.00	15.9%
Contingency	1,000.00	2.3%
Total Construction Cost	$43,370.00	100.0%
Cost Per Square Foot	$31.66	

METRO AREA: NEW YORK, NY

Finished Area (sq. ft.):	1,412
Size of Lot (sq. ft.):	1,520

SALES PRICE BREAKDOWN

Total Construction Cost	$100,964.50
Finished Lot Cost:	74,684.00
Total Financing Costs:	73, 588.00
Land Acquisition and Development Financing:	4,000.00
Construction Financing:	42,176.00
Profit, Overhead, and General Operating Expenses:	44,384.50
TOTAL SALES PRICE	$293,621.00

New York, NY

	Average	Percent of Total
Building Permits	$447.00	0.4%
Architectural	3,923.50	3.9%
Excavation/Backfill	2,344.50	2.3%
Footings/Foundation	2,407.50	2.4%
Waterproofing	647.00	0.6%
Termite Protection	-.-	-.-
Concrete Flatwork	6,918.50	6.9%
Framing for Decks/Walls	-.-	-.-
Framing for Roof	15,632.50	15.6%
Roofing	1,988.00	2.0%
Gutters/Downspouts	353.00	0.4%
Windows/Skylights	2,745.50	2.7%
Exterior Doors	276.50	0.3%
Insulation	1,299.50	1.3%
Siding/Exterior Trim	4,941.00	4.9%

HVAC	4,971.50	4.9%
Drywall	4,296.00	4.3%
Interior Painting	2,588.00	2.6%
Ceramic Tile Walls & Floors	1,945.50	1.9%
Carpet	1,447.00	1.4%
Wood Flooring	-.-	-.-
Vinyl Flooring	503.00	0.5%
Other Flooring	-.-	-.-
Interior Trim Carpentry	3,565.50	3.5%
Interior Doors	600.00	0.6%
Ceramic Tile Counter Top	-.-	-.-
Cabinets/Vanities	2,642.50	2.6%
Appliances	1,594.00	1.6%
Rough and Finish Plumbing	10,747.00	10.7%
Rough and Finish Electrical	3,439.00	3.4%
Lighting Fixtures	100.00	0.1%
Exterior Painting	788.00	0.8%
Landscaping	2,042.50	2.0%
Driveway	600.00	0.6%
Exterior Structures	1,365.00	1.4%
Final Cleanup	378.00	0.4%
Fireplace	1,470.00	1.5%
Swimming Pool	1,100.00	1.1%
Greenhouse	4,588.00	4.6%
Other	1,176.00	1.2%
Contingency	12,725.00	12.7%
Total Construction Cost	**$100,463.50**	**100.0%**
Cost Per Square Foot	$68.43	

METRO AREA: MINNEAPOLIS - ST. PAUL, MN/WI

Finished Area (sq. ft.):	2,033
Size of Lot (sq. ft.)	14,702

SALES PRICE BREAKDOWN

Total Construction Cost:	$118,850.67
Finished Lot Cost:	39,833.33
Total Financing Costs:	1,853.33
Land Acquisition and Development Financing:	1,072.50
Construction Financing:	0.00
Profit, Overhead, and General Operating Expenses:	16,881.00
TOTAL SALES PRICE	$177,418.00

Minneapolis/St. Paul, MN/WI

	Average	Percent of Total
Building Permits	$2,005.00	2.0%
Architectural	750.00	0.8%
Excavation/Backfill	2,202.50	2.2%
Footings/Foundation	5,050.00	5.1%
Waterproofing	278.33	0.3%
Termite Protection	-.-	-.-
Concrete Flatwork	20,808.00	20.9%
Framing for Decks/Walls	14,049.67	14.1%
Framing for Roof	-.-	-.-
Roofing	4,443.00	4.5%
Gutters/Downspouts	-.-	-.-
Windows/Skylights	9,004.00	9.1%
Exterior Doors	-.-	-.-
Insulation	2,490.00	2.5%
Siding/Exterior Trim	4,567.00	4.6%
HVAC	5,831.00	5.9%
Drywall	3,687.00	3.7%
Interior Painting	3,865.00	3.9%
Ceramic Tile Walls and Floors	7,085.50	7.1%
Carpet	3,097.33	3.1%
Wood Flooring	2,734.00	2.8%
Vinyl Flooring	-.-	-.-
Other Flooring	-.-	-.-
Interior Trim Carpentry	1,500.00	1.5%
Interior Doors	10,555.00	10.6%
Ceramic Tile Counter Top	2,050.00	2.1%
Cabinets/Vanities	5,696.00	5.7%
Appliances	1,416.67	1.4%
Rough and Finish Plumbing	5,545.00	5.6%
Rough and Finish Electrical	3,648.67	3.7%
Lighting Fixtures	1,566.67	1.6%
Exterior Painting	3,00.00	3.0%
Landscaping	2,077.50	2.1%
Driveway	668.00	0.7%
Exterior Structures	2,500	2.5%
Final Cleanup	558.33	0.6%
Fireplace	1,500.00	1.5%
Swimming Pool	-.-	-.-
Greenhouse	-.-	-.-
Other	-.-	-.-
Contingency	17,364.00	17.5%
Total Construction Cost	$99,353.00	100.0%
Cost Per Square Foot	$43.95	

METRO AREA: PHOENIX, AZ	
Finished Area (sq. ft.):	2,359
Size of Lot (sq. ft.):	6,800

SALES PRICE BREAKDOWN

Total Construction Cost:	$71,832.50
Finished Lot Cost:	14,400.00
Total Financing Costs:	9,525.00
Land Acquisition and Development Financing:	450.00
Construction Financing:	1,600.00
Profit, Overhead, and General Operating Expenses:	33,842.50
TOTAL SALES PRICE:	$129,150.00

Phoenix, AZ

	Average	Percent of Total
Building Permits	$2,147.00	3.2%
Architectural	-.-	-.-
Excavation/Backfill	400.00	0.6%
Footings/Foundation	1,832.00	2.7%
Waterproofing	-.-	-.-
Termite Protection	521.00	0.8%
Concrete Flatwork	4,226.00	6.3%
Framing for Decks/Walls	15,550.50	23.1%
Framing for Roof	2,900.00	4.3%
Roofing	5,170.00	7.7%
Gutters/Downspouts	-.-	-.-
Windows/Skylights	2,271.00	3.4%
Exterior Doors	560.00	0.8%
Insulation	886.50	1.3%
Siding/Exterior Trim	3,405.00	5.1%
HVAC	3,095.00	4.6%
Drywall	4,314.50	6.4%
Interior Painting	2,175.00	3.2%
Ceramic Tile Walls and Floors	3,100.00	4.6%
Carpet	1,800.00	2.7%
Wood Flooring	-.-	-.-
Vinyl Flooring	194.00	0.3%
Other Flooring	-.-	-.-
Interior Trim Carpentry	1,650.00	2.4%
Interior Doors	543.00	0.8%
Ceramic Tile Counter Top	678.00	1.0%
Cabinets/Vanities	2,775.00	4.1%
Appliances	702.50	1.0%
Rough and Finish Plumbing	3,937.50	5.8%
Rough and Finish Electrical	2,272.50	3.4%
Lighting Fixtures	309.50	0.5%
Exterior Painting	608.00	0.9%

Landscaping	247.50	0.4%
Driveway	460.00	0.7%
Exterior Structures	1,270.00	1.9%
Final Cleanup	312.50	0.5%
Fireplace	1,295.00	1.9%
Swimming Pool	7,000.00	10.4%
Greenhouse	-.-	-.-
Other	-.-	-.-
Contingency	650.00	1.0%
Total Construction Cost	$67,357.50	100.0%
Cost Per Square Foot	$28.13	

METRO AREA: ST. LOUIS, MO/IL

Finished Area (sq. ft.):	2,275
Size of Lot (sq. ft.):	6,250

SALES PRICE BREAKDOWN

Total Construction Cost:	$103,500.00
Finished Lot Cost:	28,000.00
Total Financing Costs:	4,000.00
Land Acquisition and Development Financing:	1,500.00
Construction Financing:	2,500.00
Profit, Overhead, and General Operating Expenses:	28,000.00
TOTAL SALES PRICE:	$163,500.00

St. Louis, MO/IL

	Average	Percent of Total
Building Permits	$350.00	0.3%
Architectural	3,800.00	3.1%
Excavation/Backfill	2,800.00	2.3%
Footings/Foundation	25,651.50	20.8%
Waterproofing	473.00	0.4%
Termite Protection	110.00	0.1%
Concrete Flatwork	4,834.00	3.9%
Framing for Decks/Walls	19,607.50	15.9%
Framing for Roof	1,868.00	1.5%
Roofing	1,904.50	1.5%
Gutters/Downspouts	500.00	0.4%
Windows/Skylights	3,000.00	2.4%
Exterior Doors	1,234.00	1.0%
Insulation	1,392.50	1.1%
Siding/Exterior Trim	4,422.00	3.6%

HVAC	4,030.00	3.3%
Drywall	5,916.50	4.8%
Interior Painting	3,438.00	2.8%
Ceramic Tile Walls and Floors	2,238.00	1.8%
Carpet	-.-	-.-
Wood Flooring	-.-	-.-
Vinyl Flooring	-.-	-.-
Other Flooring	-.-	-.-
Interior Trim Carpentry	7,917.50	6.4%
Interior Doors	4,730.50	6.4%
Ceramic Tile Counter Top	-.-	-.-
Cabinets/Vanities	3,649.50	3.0%
Appliances	1,353.00	1.1%
Rough and Finish Plumbing	6,268.50	5.1%
Rough and Finish Electrical	3,530.00	2.9%
Lighting Fixtures	700.00	0.6%
Exterior Painting	-.-	-.-
Landscaping	3,700.00	3.0%
Driveway	3,850.00	3.1%
Exterior Structures	-.-	-.-
Final Cleanup	222.50	0.2%
Fireplace	1,154.50	0.9%
Swimming Pool	-.-	-.-
Greenhouse	-.-	-.-
Other	4,100.00	3.3%
Contingency	6,715.00	5.5%
Total Construction Cost	123,050.50	100.0%
Cost Per Square Foot	$55.36	

METRO AREA: SAN DIEGO, CA

Finished Area (sq. ft.):	2,897
Size of Lot (sq. ft):	10,667

SALES PRICE BREAKDOWN

Total Construction Cost:	$123,856.00
Finished Lot Cost:	97,132.00
Total Financing Costs:	18,062.33
Land Acquisition and Development Financing:	4,281.50
Construction Financing:	13,812.00
Profit, Overhead, and General Operating Expenses:	73,378.00
TOTAL SALES PRICE:	$312,428.33

San Diego, CA

	Average	Percent of Total
Building Permits	$7,453.00	6.3%
Architectural	1,091.67	0.9%
Excavation/Backfill	2,250.00	1.9%
Footings/Foundation	10,497.33	8.8%
Waterproofing	450.00	0.4%
Termite Protection	-.-	-.-
Concrete Flatwork	600.00	0.5%
Framing for Decks/Walls	26,900.00	22.6%
Framing for Roof	-.-	-.-
Roofing	4,158.33	3.5%
Gutters/Downspouts	2,500.00	2.1%
Windows/Skylights	2,544.00	2.1%
Exterior Doors	1,025.00	0.9%
Insulation	1,283.33	1.1%
Siding/Exterior Trim	10,773.00	9.1%
HVAC	2,785.33	2.3%
Drywall	7,765.67	6.5%
Interior Painting	3,141.00	2.6%
Ceramic Tile Walls and Floors	1,947.50	1.6%
Carpet	4,115.00	3.5%
Wood Flooring	—	—
Vinyl Flooring	425.00	0.4%
Other Flooring	3,328.00	2.8%
Interior Trim Carpentry	4,427.00	3.7%
Interior Doors	1,480.50	1.2%
Ceramic Tile Counter Top	3,453.33	2.9%
Cabinets/Vanities	3,964.00	3.3%
Appliances	1,980.00	1.7%
Rough and Finish Plumbing	7,402.67	6.2%
Rough and Finish Electrical	3,184.00	2.7%
Lighting Fixtures	714.33	0.6%
Exterior Painting	200.00	0.2%
Landscaping	2,385.00	2.0%
Driveway	3,583.33	3.0%
Exterior Structures	3,550.00	3.0%
Final Cleanup	994.67	0.8%
Fireplace	1,415.00	1.2%
Swimming Pool	—	—
Greenhouse	—	—
Other	2,360.00	2.0%
Contingency	650.00	0.5%
Total Construction Cost	$119,030.67	100.0%
Cost Per Square Foot	$40.11	

METRO AREA: TULSA, OK

Finished Area (sq. ft.):	2,277
Size of Lot (sq. ft.):	25,233

SALES PRICE BREAKDOWN

Total Construction Cost:	$67,923.67
Finished Lot Cost:	15,000.00
Total Financing Costs:	3,800.00
Land Acquisition and Development Financing:	N/A
Construction Financing:	4,100.00
Profit, Overhead, and General Operating Expenses:	15,933.33
TOTAL SALES PRICE:	$102,657.00

Tulsa, OK

	Average	Percent of Total
Building Permits	$604.33	1.0%
Architectural	543.33	0.9%
Excavation/Backfill	1,166.67	1.9%
Footings/Foundation	2,591.67	4.2%
Waterproofing	–.–	–.–
Termite Protection	325.00	0.5%
Concrete Flatwork	1,865.00	3.0%
Framing for Decks/Walls	14,000.00	22.6%
Framing for Roof	4,250.00	6.9%
Roofing	1,762.33	2.8%
Gutters/Downspouts	800.00	1.3%
Windows/Skylights	1,732.67	2.8%
Exterior Doors	951.33	1.5%
Insulation	1,369.67	2.2%
Siding/Exterior Trim	2,300.00	3.7%
HVAC	3,980.00	6.4%
Drywall	3,297.00	5.3%
Interior Painting	2,950.00	4.8%
Ceramic Tile Walls and Floors	1,691.67	5.8%
Carpet	3,616.67	5.8%
Wood Flooring	675.00	1.1%
Vinyl Flooring	961.67	1.6%
Other Flooring	–.–	–.–
Interior Trim Carpentry	2,567.00	4.1%
Interior Doors	1,525.00	2.5%
Ceramic Tile Counter Top	450.00	0.7%
Cabinets/Vanities	3,755.00	6.1%
Appliances	1,529.00	2.5%
Rough and Finish Plumbing	3,660.00	5.9%
Rough and Finish Electrical	2,933.33	4.7%
Lighting Fixtures	1,050.00	1.7%
Exterior Painting	1,000.00	1.6%

Landscaping	750.00	1.2%
Driveway	1,776.67	2.9%
Exterior Structures	-.-	-.-
Final Cleanup	296.67	0.5%
Fireplace	1,616.67	2.6%
Swimming Pool	-.-	-.-
Greenhouse	-.-	-.-
Other	6,971.00	11.2%
Contingency	-.-	-.-
Total Construction Cost	$61,970.33	100.0%
Cost Per Square Foot	$27.38	

METRO AREA: WEST PALM BEACH, FL

Finished Area (sq. ft.):	2,000
Size of Lot (sq. ft.):	10,200

SALES PRICE BREAKDOWN

Total Construction Cost:	$98,000.00
Finished Lot Cost:	22,000.00
Total Financing Costs:	0.00
Land Acquisition and Development Financing:	0.00
Construction Financing:	0.00
Profit, Overhead, and General Operating Expenses:	12,000.00
TOTAL SALES PRICE:	$132,000.00

West Palm Beach, FL

	Average	Percent of Total
Building Permits	$1,000.00	0.9%
Architectural	2,000.00	1.8%
Excavation/Backfill	2,000.00	1.8%
Footings/Foundation	3,000.00	2.8%
Waterproofing	-.-	-.-
Termite Protection	100.00	0.1%
Concrete Flatwork	800.00	0.7%
Framing for Decks/Walls	9,000.00	8.3%
Framing for Roof	7,500.00	6.9%
Roofing	2,500.00	2.3%
Gutters/Downspouts	-.-	-.-
Windows/Skylights	2,500.00	2.3%
Exterior Doors	1,500.00	1.4%
Insulation	1,000.00	0.9%
Siding/Exterior Trim	3,500.00	3.2%

HVAC	3,500.00	3.2%
Drywall	3,000.00	2.8%
Interior Painting	1,500.00	1.4%
Ceramic Tile Walls and Floors	2,500.00	2.3%
Carpet	2,500.00	2.3%
Wood Flooring	-.-	-.-
Vinyl Flooring	-.-	-.-
Other Flooring	-.-	-.-
Interior Trim Carpentry	600.00	0.6%
Interior Doors	1,000.00	0.9%
Ceramic Tile Counter Top	-.-	-.-
Cabinets/Vanities	7,000.00	6.4%
Appliances	1,500.00	1.4%
Rough and Finish Plumbing	5,000.00	4.6%
Rough and Finish Electrical	4,500.00	4.1%
Lighting Fixtures	1,000.00	0.9%
Exterior Painting	1,500.00	1.4%
Landscaping	2,000.00	1.8%
Driveway	1,500.00	1.4%
Exterior Structures	-.-	-.-
Final Cleanup	200.00	0.2%
Fireplace	3,000.00	2.8%
Swimming Pool	20,000.00	18.4%
Greenhouse	5,000.00	4.6%
Other	-.-	-.-
Contingency	5,500.00	5.1%
Total Construction Cost	$108,700.00	100.0%
Cost Per Square Foot	$54.35	

All cost charts are taken from "Construction Costs by Metro Area" (September 1990), courtesy of the Economics Department of the National Association of Home Builders.

Conclusion

There are many kinds of "manufactured housing," including log and timber homes, pre-cut or panelized homes, modular homes, and manufactured homes. In this book, we have concentrated on *affordable housing* only. Log and timber homes (the subject of another book) are beautiful but are more expensive per square foot than ordinary site-built homes, and certainly more expensive than manufactured or modular homes (homes that are built completely in the factory and delivered completely finished, perhaps even totally or partially furnished, to the buyer). Like log and timber homes, pre-cut or panelized homes require on-site assembly, and while some economies in labor costs may be possible, depending on your own building skills, you must usually hire significant quantities of on-site labor, which again may affect affordability.

CHANGING THE PREVAILING ATTITUDES

Our nation's elected officials often profess a concern for the common person, the working class, and the elderly. But the record of the nation for over-regulating housing and thus driving up housing costs stands in stark contrast to the voiced concerns. Someone has recently pointed out that the Empire State Building was built in one year: today, it would take five years to get the permits approved and to file the environmental impact statement. The story may be apocryphal but the facts remain: delays of months or years in approving a community development will add greatly to the final cost of the project, through annual inflation alone. We must somehow have a breakthrough in the bureaucracy and red tape that cause endless and expensive delay in zoning, planning, and development.

Jack Kemp, Secretary of Housing and Urban Development (HUD), has stated that "needless rules, red tape, and the 'not in my back yard syndrome' are pushing prices beyond the reach of most Americans who should be able to afford homes." Referring to a housing report by the Advisory Commission on Regulatory Barriers to Affordable Housing, titled "Not In My Back Yard, Removing Barriers to Affordable Housing," Kemp says: "Housing is one of the most over-regulated industries in this country. This report will trigger a significant rethinking of regulations that have put housing almost out of reach of the poor. We've got to balance between the regulatory process, the tax code, the environment and the ultimate enemy, which is the 'not in my back yard' or NIMBY syndrome." In Chapter 7, we listed some of the barriers that can impede the development of manufactured housing.

SUBSIDIZING PEOPLE, NOT HOUSES

Years ago, an economist pointed out that federal government programs subsidized *houses*, when the solution to housing the nation would be to subsidize *people*. By this he meant that government programs often paid builders to build entire communities to house the poor, and in doing so often succeeded only in creating instant slums. This economist proposed that a better solution would be to send the affected family a subsidy check each month, and let the family seek out their own housing, rather than directing the family to a "welfare community." I am in favor of that approach. The problem is, when the family sets out with a housing check in hand (either earned or subsidized income), there are often so many barriers to affordable housing that the family may not be able to spend the check.

As Secretary Kemp points out, the "ultimate enemy is the 'not in my back yard' syndrome" on the part of the public. In an election year in which the public has expressed anger over the high cost of government, we should all ponder the fact that we pay more taxes because we prohibit the development of affordable housing, and thus force governmental agencies to seek more expensive alternatives to house people. It may seem odd to many of us to realize that until the Fair Housing Act of 1988, local restrictions in many cases denied a family with children the right to live in a manufactured home.

HOUSING SUBSIDIES FOR THOSE WHO NEED THEM

Many of us might wonder about the lack of affordable housing, given all the housing subsidies discussed in the news media. Keep in mind that the subsidies are aimed generally at the middle and upper classes: those who contribute to politicians and who vote to elect them. For the middle class to the rich, there are low-interest loans, with low or no down payments, via FHA and GI programs. There is the tax deductible aspect of mortgage interest payments, and of local property taxes, for the middle class. The wealthy often are more heavily subsidized than the middle class, because their mortgages and deductions are larger, and often they can even deduct a second home. In the meantime, the working single mother who is paying rent has no mortgage interest or property taxes to deduct, and must pay higher interest rates for a mortgage — assuming she can come up with the higher down payment that is often required of her. Nor is affordable housing a concern only for the poor. Most housing programs that promote home ownership are aimed at the person in the upper 70 percent income bracket.

AFFORDABLE HOUSING WORKS

A first step to housing all the people would be to make possible the development of more communities for affordable housing, plus following the lead of the California legislature in their passage of the Fair Zoning Legislation, to make all single-family residential lots available for manufactured housing.

In communities where government, financial institutions, and developers have cooperated, manufactured housing has been made to work. In Chapter 8, Community Development, we have cited progress in Washington, in California, and in suburban Detroit, Michigan. The result has been only a beneficial increase in the availability of affordable housing for the first-time buyer, the single person, the retiree, and migrant and farm workers. There are numerous examples for developers in all cities to follow. Clearly we have the resources to provide adequate housing for all; just as clearly we have lacked the will to do so.

Appendices

1. Manufacturers

AMERICAN FAMILY HOMES, INC.
Highway 71 North
P.O. Box 438
Anderson, MO
Ms. Ann Taylor, Personnel Director
(417) 845-3311
Fax: (417) 845-3315

BAYSHORE HOMES OF CALIFORNIA, INC.
11 N. County Road 101
Box 1427
Woodland, CA 95695
Mr. Thomas Bryant, President
(916) 662-9621
Fax: (916) 661-1179

BELLCREST HOMES, INC.
206 Magnolia Street
P.O. Box 630
Millen, GA 30442
Mr. Glinn H. Spann, President
(912) 982-4000
Fax: (912) 982-2992

BRIGADIER HOMES OF NORTH CAROLINA, INC.
P.O. Box 1007
Highway 64 East
Nashville, NC 27856
Mr. Tony Castle, General Manager
(919) 459-7026
Fax: (919) 459-7529

BUCCANEER HOMES OF ALABAMA, INC.
P.O. Box 1418
Hamilton, AL 35570
Mr. Charles Demsey, President
(205) 921-3135
Fax: (205) 921-7390

BURLINGTON HOMES OF NEW ENGLAND, INC.
P.O. Box 263
Route 26
Oxford, ME 04270
Mr. Jack Ireton-Hewitt, President
(207) 539-4406
Fax: (207) 539-2900

CAVALIER HOMES, INC.
P.O. Box 300
Highway 41 North
Addison, AL 35540
Mr. James Caldwell
(205) 747-1575
Fax: (205) 747-2107

CHAMPION HOME BUILDERS COMPANY
5573 North Street
Dryden, MI 48428
Mr. Joseph J. Morris
(313) 694-3195
Fax: (313) 796-2145

CHIEF INDUSTRIES INC.
Bonavilla Homes
P.O. Box 127
West Highway 34
Aurora, NE 68818
Mr. Melvin Auch, President
(402) 694-5250

CLAYTON HOMES, INC.
P.O. Box 15169
Knoxville, TN 37901
Mr. James L. Clayton
Chief Executive Officer
(615) 970-7200
Fax: (615) 970-1238

THE COMMODORE CORPORATION
P.O. Box 577
Goshen, IN 46526
Mr. Thomas L. Underwood
President
(219) 533-7100
Fax: (219) 534-2716

CRESTLINE HOMES
Route 3, Box 67
Laurinburg, NC 28352
Mr. Joe Manis
President
(919) 276-0195
Fax: (919) 276-7989

FISHER CORPORATION
P.O. Box 1000
Highway 52
Richfield, NC 28137
Mr. Jacob E. Fisher, Jr.
(704) 463-1341
Fax: (704) 463-5199

FLEETWOOD ENTERPRISES
3125 Myers Street
P.O. Box 7638
Riverside, CA 92523
Mr. Glenn F. Kummer, President
(714) 351-3500
Fax: (714) 351-3776

FRANKLIN HOMES, INC.
Route 3, Box 207
Russellville, AL 35653
Mr. Jerry James, President
(205) 332-4510 ext. 30
Fax: (205) 332-5449

FUQUA HOMES, INC.
7100 South Cooper
Arlington, TX 76017
Mr. William C. Noble, President
(817) 465-3211
Fax: (817) 465-5125

GATEWAY HOMES
P.O. Box 728
Guin, AL 35563
Mr. Tex Johnson, President
(205) 468-3191
Fax: (205) 468-3336

GOLDEN WEST HOMES, INC.
1308 E. Wakeham
Santa Ana, CA 92705
Mr. Robert J. Henry, Senior Vice President
(714) 835-4200
Fax: (714) 835-6232

GUERDON INDUSTRIES, INC.
5285 S.W. Meadows
Suite 315
Lake Oswego, OR 97035
Mr. Al Preusch, President
(503) 624-6400
Fax: (503) 620-5929

HOMECORP, INC.
19224 C.R. #8
Bristol, IN 46507
Mr. Russell Peterson, Chairman & CEO
(219) 848-4421
Fax: (219) 848-5755

KEISER HOMES OF MAINE
P.O. Box 470
Oxford, ME 04270
Mr. Don Longstreet, President
(207) 539-8883
Fax: (207) 539-4446

KIT MANUFACTURING COMPANY
P.O. Box 848
Long Beach, CA 90801
Mr. Dan Pocapalia, Chairman, President & CEO
(213) 595-7451
Fax: (213) 426-8463

MANSION HOMES
P.O. Box 39
Plank Road
Robbins, NC 27325
Mr. Don Fox, General Manager
(919) 948-2141
Fax: (919) 948-3752

MOBILE HOME ESTATES, INC.
Route #4
Bryan, OH 43506
Mr. Nathan E. Kimpel, Vice President
(419) 636-4511
Fax: (419) 636-9144

MODULINE INTERNATIONAL, INC.
P.O. Box 3000
205 College Street, S.E.
Lacey, WA 98503
Mr. L.C. Merta, President
(206) 491-1130
Fax: (206) 491-1135

OAKWOOD HOMES CORPORATION
P.O. Box 7386
Greensboro, NC 27417-0386
Mr. Nicholas J. St. George, President & CEO
(919) 855-2400 ext. 2342
Fax: (919) 852-1537

PATRIOT HOMES, INC.
57420 C.R. #3, South
Elkhart, IN 46517
Mr. Samuel Weidner, President
(219) 293-6507
Fax: (219) 522-2339

PEACH STATE HOMES
P.O. Box 615
Adel, GA 31620
Mr. Roger D. Watson, President
(912) 896-7420
Fax: (912) 896-2575

R-ANELL CUSTOM HOMES
P.O. Box 428
Denver, NC 28037
Mr. Rollan Jones, President
(704) 483-5511
Fax: (704) 483-5674

REDMAN HOMES, INC.
2550 Walnut Hill Lane
Suite 200
Dallas, TX 75229
Mr. Skip Miller, Division Vice President
(214) 353-3600 ext. 639
Fax: (214) 956-9986

ROCHESTER HOMES INC.
East Lucas Street
P.O. Box 587
Rochester, IN 46975
Mr. Milam Anderson, President
(219) 223-4321
Fax: (219) 862-2239

SCHULT HOMES CORPORATION
P.O. Box 251
221 U.S. 20 West
Middlebury, IN 46540
Mr. Walter Wells, President
(219) 825-5881
Fax: (800) 955-2355

SUN BELT ENERGY HOUSING
Highway 5 North
P.O. Box 340
Haleyville, AL 35565
Jerry Perkins, Vice President & General Manager
(205) 486-9535
Fax: (205) 486-4197

SKYLINE CORPORATION
P.O. Box 743
Elkhart, IN 46515
Mr. Arthus J. Decio, Chairman & CEO
(219) 294-6521
Fax: (219) 293-7574

SUNSHINE HOMES, INC.
P.O. Box 507
Red Bay, AL 35582
Mr. John Bostick, President
(205) 356-4427
Fax: (205) 356-9694

VICTORIAN HOMES, INC.
P.O. Box 707
11948 C.R. #14
Middlebury, IN 36540
Mr. Dennis Beadle, President
(219) 825-5841
Fax: (219) 825-9851

VIRGINIA HOMES MFG. CORP.
P.O. Box 410
Boydton, VA 23917
Mr. Roger L. Mitchell, President & CEO
(804) 738-6107
Fax: (804) 738-6926

WESTWAY HOMES, INC.
P.O. Box 3850
Ontario, CA 91761
Mr. Robert N. West, Vice President
(714) 947-3816
Fax: (714) 947-2307

WICK BUILDING SYSTEMS, INC.
404 Walter Road
P.O. Box 490
Mazomanie, WI 53560-0490
Mr. Jeff Wick, President & CEO
(608) 795-4281
Fax: (608) 795-2740

2. State Manufactured Housing Associations

Following is a list of manufactured housing state associations. If you are in search of a dealer or a manufacturer of homes, your first step may be to contact your own state's manufactured housing association for a list of dealers or manufacturers near you. For any further information about manufactured housing, please contact your state association or the Manufactured Housing Institute in Washington, DC. (See end of list for address and phone number of the MHI.)

Alabama
Alabama Housing Institute, Inc.
400 South Union Street, Suite 485
Montgomery, AL 36104
Allen Moore, Executive Director
(205) 264-8755
Fax: (205) 834-6398

Arizona
Manufactured Housing Industry of Arizona
1801 Jen Tilly Lane, #B-10
Tempe, AZ 85281
Gub Mix, Executive Director
(602) 966-9221

Arkansas
Arkansas Manufactured Housing Association
2500 McCain Place, Suite 203
N. Little Rock, AR 72116
Katherine O'Bryan, Executive Director
(501) 771-0444
Fax: (501) 771-0445

California
California Manufactured Housing Institute
10390 Commerce Center Drive, Suite 130
Rancho Cucamonga, CA 91730
Jess Maxcy, President
(714) 987-2599
Fax: (714) 989-0434

Western Mobilehome Association
1760 Creekside Oaks Drive, Suite 200
Sacramento, CA 95833
David Milton, Executive Director
(916) 641-7002
Fax: (916) 641-7006

Colorado
Colorado Manufactured Housing Association
2074 South Utica
Denver, CO 80219
LeMoyne C. Brown, Executive Vice President
(303) 935-8943

Connecticut
New England Manufactured Housing Association, Inc.
167 Milk Street, Suite 408
Boston, MA 02109
Robert Howe
Executive Director
(508) 832-0642
Fax: (508) 832-0643

Delaware
Delaware Manufactured Housing Association
Treadway Towers, Suite 309
Dover, DE 19901
Marcene A. Gory
Executive Director
(302) 678-2588
Fax: (302) 678-4767

Florida
Florida Manufactured Housing Association
115 North Calhoun, Suite 5
Tallahassee, FL 32301
Frank Williams
Executive Director
(904) 222-4011
Fax: (904) 222-7957

Georgia

Georgia Manufactured Housing Association
1000 Circle 75 Parkway
Suite 060
Atlanta, GA 30339
Charlotte Gattis, Executive Director
(404) 955-4522
Fax: (404) 955-5575

Idaho

Idaho Manufactured Housing Association
3180-1 E. Desert Inn Road #165
Las Vegas, NV 89121
Gub Mix, President
(702) 737-7778
Fax: (702) 737-0299

Illinois

Illinois Manufactured Housing Association
3888 Peoria Road
Indianapolis, IN 62702
Mike Marlowe, Executive Director
(217) 528-3423
Fax: (217) 544-4642

Indiana

Indiana Manufactured Housing Association
3210 Rand Road
Indianapolis, IN 46241
Connie Moore, Executive Vice President
(317) 247-6258
Fax: (317) 243-9174

Iowa

Manufactured Housing Association of Iowa
1400 Dean Avenue
Des Moines, IA 50316
Joe Kelly, Executive Vice President
(515) 265-1497
Fax: (515) 265-6480

Kansas

Kansas Manufactured Housing Institute
112 SW 6th Street, Suite 204

Topeka, KS 66603
Terry Humphrey, Executive Director
(913) 357-5256
Fax: (913) 357-5257

Kentucky

Kentucky Manufactured Housing Institute
2170 U.S. Route 127 South
Frankfort, KY 40601
Bill Young, Executive Director
(502) 223-0490
Fax: (502) 223-7305

Louisiana

Louisiana Manufactured Housing Association
4847 Revere Avenue
Baton Rouge, LA 70808
Steve Duke, Executive Director
(504) 925-9041
Fax: (504) 926-0119

Maine

Manufactured Housing Association of Maine
Two Central Plaza
Augusta, ME 04330
Robert Howe, Executive Director
(207) 622-4406
Fax: (207) 622-4437

Maryland

Maryland Manufactured Housing Association
P.O. Box 2185
Annapolis, MD 21404
Leonard S. Homa, Executive Director
(301) 956-2663

Massachusetts

New England Manufactured Housing Association,
    Inc.
167 Milk Street, Suite 408
Boston, MA 02109
Robert Howe, Executive Director
(508) 832-0642
Fax: (508) 832-0643

Michigan

Michigan Manufactured Housing Association
2123 University Park Drive, Suite 110
Okemos, MI 48864
Tim DeWitt, Executive Director
(517) 349-3300
Fax: (517) 349-3543

Minnesota

Minnesota Manufactured Housing Association
555 Park Street, Suite 400
Saint Paul, MN 55103
Mark Brunner, Executive Vice President
(612) 222-6789
Fax: (612) 222-6913

Mississippi

Mississippi Manufactured Housing Association
P.O. Box 668
Jackson, MS 39205-0668
Thad Vann, Executive Director
(601) 355-1879

Missouri

Missouri Manufactured Housing Institute
502 Mulberry, P.O. Box 1365
Jefferson City, MO 65101
Joyce Baker, Executive Director
(314) 636-8660
Fax: (314) 636-4912

Montana

Montana Manufactured Housing Association
350 Last Chance Gulch
Helena, MT 59601
Stuart Doggett, Executive Director
(406) 442-2164

Nebraska

Nebraska Manufactured Housing Institute, Inc.
211 North 12th Street, Suite 400
Lincoln, NE 68508
Alan Wood, Executive Director
(402) 475-3675
Fax: (402) 476-0543

Nevada

Nevada Manufactured Housing Association
3180-1 E. Desert Inn Road, #165
Las Vegas, NV 89121
Gub Mix
Executive Director
(702) 737-7778
Fax: (702) 737-0299

New Hampshire

New England Manufactured Housing Association,
   Inc.
167 Milk Street, Suite 408
Boston, MA 02109
Robert Howe, Executive Director
(508) 832-0642
Fax: (508) 832-0643

New Jersey

New Jersey Manufactured Housing Association
2382 Whitehorse-Mercerville Road
Trenton, NJ 08619
Judith A. Thornton
Executive Director
(609) 588-9040
Fax: (609) 588-9041

New Mexico

Manufactured Housing Foundation
   (of New Mexico)
P.O. Box 11607
Albuquerque, NM 87192-0607
Bill Branscum
Executive Director
(505) 299-4070
Fax: (505) 296-5193

New York

New York Manufactured Housing Association, Inc.
421 New Karner Road
Albany, NY 12205-3809
Barbara Faraone
Executive Director
(518) 464-5087
Fax: (518) 464-5096

North Carolina

North Carolina Manufactured Housing Institute
P.O. Box 95132
Raleigh, NC 27625
Steve Zamiara, Executive Director
(919) 872-2740
Fax: (919) 872-4826

North Dakota

North Dakota Manufactured Housing Association
P.O. Box 2681
Bismarck, ND 58502
John Dwyer, Executive Vice President
(701) 224-1266

Ohio

Ohio Manufactured Housing Association
906 East Broad Street
Columbus, OH 43205
James Ayotte, Executive Director
(614) 258-6642
Fax: (614) 258-7488

Oklahoma

Manufactured Housing Association of Oklahoma
P.O. Box 32309
Oklahoma City, OK 73123
Jim Shaver, Executive Director
(405) 521-8470
Fax: (405) 720-0451

Oregon

Oregon Manufactured Housing Association
2255 State Street
Salem, OR 97301
Don Miner, Executive Director
(503) 364-2470
Fax: (503) 371-7374

Pennsylvania

Pennsylvania Manufactured Housing Association
P.O. Box 248
New Cumberland, PA 17070
Jim Moore, Executive Vice President
(717) 774-3440
Fax: (717) 774-5596

Rhode Island

New England Manufactured Housing Association, Inc.
167 Milk Street, Suite 408
Boston, MA 02109
Robert Howe, Executive Director
(508) 832-0642
Fax: (508) 832-0643

South Carolina

Manufactured Housing Institute of South Carolina
P.O. Box 5885
West Columbia, SC 29171-5885
Steve Rogers, Executive Director
(803) 794-5570
Fax: (803) 794-4247

South Dakota

South Dakota Manufactured Housing Association
P.O. Box 756
Mitchell, SD 57301
Dean E. Wieczorek, Executive Director

Tennessee

Tennessee Manufactured Housing Association
240 Great Circle Road, Suite 332
Nashville, TN 37228
Bonita Hamm, Executive Director
(615) 256-4733 or 4741
Fax: (615) 255-8869

Texas

Texas Manufactured Housing Association
2215 E. Anderson Lane
P.O. Box 14428
Austin, TX 78761
Will Ehrle, President & General Counsel
(512) 459-1222
Fax: (512) 459-1511

Utah

Utah Manufactured Housing Association
3180-1 E. Desert Inn Road, #165
Las Vegas, NV 89121
Gub Mix, Executive Director
(702) 737-7778
Fax: (702) 737-0299

Vermont
New England Manufactured Housing Association,
    Inc.
167 Milk Street, Suite 408
Boston, MA 02109
Robert Howe, Executive Director
(508) 832-0642
Fax: (508) 832-0643

Virginia
Virginia Manufactured Housing Association
4435 Waterfront Drive, #103
Glen Allen, VA 23060
Ron Dunlap, Executive Director
(804) 747-0810
Fax: (804) 270-2049

Washington
Washington Manufactured Housing Association
P.O. Box 621
Olympia, WA 98507
Joan Brown, Executive Director
(206) 357-5650
Fax: (206) 357-5651

West Virginia
West Virginia Manufactured Housing Association
205 First Avenue
Nitro, WV 25143
Leff Moore, Executive Director
(304) 727-7431 Office & Fax

Wisconsin
Wisconsin Manufactured Housing Association
217 South Hamilton Street
Suite 301
Madison, WI 53703
Ross Kinzler, Executive Director

Wyoming
Wyoming Manufactured Housing Association
P.O. Box 1896
Cheyenne, WY 82003
Leonard Sullivan, Executive Director
(307) 635-0047

National Headquarters
Manufactured Housing Institute
1745 Jefferson Davis Highway, Suite 511
Arlington, VA 22202
Bruce Savage, Director of Public Relations
(703) 979-6620
Fax: (703) 486-0938

3. Modular Building Systems Council

The Modular Building Systems Council is a national organization of manufacturers of modular buildings. The following list includes the name and address of the manufacturer, phone number, and sales contact person. Contact individual manufacturers for information on design, floor plans and specifications, and builder/dealers in your area. The following list is provided by and courtesy of the Building Systems Councils of the National Association of Home Builders, 1201 15th Street, NW, Washington, DC 20005.

A.S.I. OF NEW YORK, INC.
5911 Loomis Road
Farmington, NY 14425
(716) 924-7151
Fax: (716) 924-4804
Contact: Frank Orr
Building Types: single-family, multi-family
Market Area: NY, MA, CT, NH, VT

ACTIVE HOMES CORPORATION
7938 South Van Dyke
Marlette, MI 48453
(517) 635-3532
Fax: (517) 635-3327
Contact: Alan Froehle, Executive Director
Sales: Dick McHugh
Building Types: single-family, multi-family
Market Area: MI, worldwide

ALL AMERICAN HOMES, INC.
1418 S. 13th Street
Decatur, IN 46733
(219) 724-9171
(219) 875-2421
Fax: (219) 724-8987
Contact: Larry Bultemeier, President
Sales: Jim Jackson, Jerry Rouch
Building Types: single-family, multi-family
Market Area: Mid-West

Other Plant Locations:
Box 219
Dyersville, LA 52040
(319) 875-2421
Contact: Mike Breen, VP/Gen. Mgr.

ALOUETTE HOMES
P.O. Box 187
Newport, VT 05855
(514) 539-3100
Fax: (514) 539-0335
Contact: Bradley Berneche, President
Building Types: single-family, multi-family, commercial
Market Area: New England and NY

AVIS HOMES CO.
Henry Street
Avis, PA 17721
(717) 753-3700
(800) 233-3052
Fax: (717) 753-3291
Contact: Martin J. Ferrario, President
Sales: Thomas Hetherington
Building Types: single-family, multi-family
Market Area: Mid-Atlantic

BEAVER MOUNTAIN LOG HOMES, INC.
RD 1, Box 32
Hancock, NY 13783
(607) 467-2700
(800) 233-2700
Fax: (607) 467-2715
Contact: Kenneth Clark, VP
Building Types: single-family, multi-family, commercial
Market Area: U.S. and Japan

BRADBURY CORPORATION
111 Frontage Road, South
Pacific, WA 98047
(206) 833-3113
Fax: (206) 833-3141
Contact Douglas A. Steinhauer, President
Sales: Bill Powers (Consumers)
Douglas Steinhauer (Builders)
Building Types: single-family, multi-family, commercial
Market Area: WA, ID, AK

CARDINAL HOMES, INC.
P.O. Box 10
Wylliesburg, VA 23976
(804) 735-8111
Fax: (804) 735-8824
Contact: D.J. Cappaert, President
Building Types: single-family
Market Area: MD, DE, VA, WV, NC

CONTEMPRI HOMES, INC.
Stauffer Industrial Park
Taylor, PA 18517-9601
(717) 562-0110
Fax: (717) 562-0737
Contact: George West, President
Sales: Michael Zangardi, VP of Sales
Building Types: single-family, multi-family, commercial
Market Area: Mid-Atlantic and New England

Other Plant Locations:
Stauffer Industrial Park
Taylor, PA 18517-9601
Contact: Robert Owsley, Gen. Mgr.

CUSTOMIZED STRUCTURES, INC.
P.O. Box 884, Plains Road
Claremont, NH 03743
(603) 543-1236
Fax: (603) 542-5650
Contact: Joseph Landers, President
Sales: Lawrence E. Haiman, VP Sales
Building Types: single-family, multi-family, commercial
Market Area: New England and NY

DKMBE MANUFACTURERS
P.O Box 325, Rt. 442E
Muncy, PA 17756
(717) 546-2261
Fax: (717) 546-5868
Contact: Thomas Saltsgiver, President
Sales: L. Robert Bellmore, Dir. of Mktg.
Building Types: single-family, multi-family, commercial
Market Area: Eastern U.S.

Other Plant Locations:
Superior Builders
P.O. Box 344, Rt. 442E
Muncy, PA 17756
(717) 546-2264
Fax: (717) 546-2266
Contact: Dennis Morgan, Gen. Mgr.

Muncy Homes
P.O. Box 325, Rt 442E
Muncy, PA 17756
(717) 546-2261
Fax: (717) 546-5898
Contact: Michael Clementoni, Gen. Mgr.

Advanced Building Technology
P.O. Box 467
1 American Drive
Tamaqua, PA 18252
(717) 668-5670
Fax: (717) 668-6454
Contact: Al Paris, Gen. Mgr.

Premier Builders
P.O. Box 337, Rt 442E
Muncy, PA 17756
(717) 546-8915
Fax: (717) 546-5898
Contact: Richard Shives, Gen. Mgr.

Muncy Homes of North Carolina
P.O. Box 1150
Webb Road
Ellenboro, NC 28040
(704) 453-0711
Contact: Clarence Stephenson, Gen. Mgr.

DELUXE HOMES OF PA, INC.
499 West Third Street
P.O. Box 323
Berwick, PA 18603
(717) 752-5914
Fax: (717) 752-6904
Contact: Don Shiner, VP Marketing and Sales
Sales: Ron Minakowski: Single-family sales
Tom Aten, Multi-family sales
Building Types: single-family, multi-family, wood and
    steelframe construction
Market Area: Mid-Atlantic, New England

DESIGN HOMES, INC.
P.O. Box 411
West 5th Street
Mifflinville, PA 18631
(717) 752-1001
Fax: (717) 752-1013

DYNAMIC HOMES, INC.
525 Roosevelt Avenue
Detroit Lakes, MN 56501
(218) 847-2661
Fax: (218) 847-2661
Contact: Vern Muzik, Exec. VP
Building Types: single-family, multi-family, commercial
Market Area: IA, MN, ND, SD, WI

EPOCH CORPORATION
P.O. Box 235
Pembroke, NH 03275
(603) 225-3907
Fax: (603) 225-8329
Contact: Douglas Basnett, President
Sales: Jack Donnelly
Building Types: single-family, multi-family
Market Area: New England, Eastern NY

FUTURE HOME TECHNOLOGY, INC., THE
P.O. Box 4255
33 Ralph Street
Port Jervis, NY 12771
(914) 856-9033
Fax: (914) 858-2488
Contact: James Gorton, Gen. Mgr.
Sales: Joseph Cappelli, VP Sales
Building Types: single-family, multi-family
Market Area: New England, NY, NJ, PA, MD, VA, WV

GENERAL HOUSING CORP.
900 Andre Street
Bay City, MI 48706
(517) 684-8078
Fax: (517) 684-4333
Contact: Bradford Light, President
Sales: John Pollion, VP Sales
Building Types: single-family, multi-family, commercial
Market Area: MI, OH, IN, Ontario

Other Plant Locations:
4644 Fraser Road
Bay City, MI 48706
(517) 684-2770

GLEN RIVER INDUSTRIES
1703 Lum Road
Centralia, WA 98531
(206) 736-1341, Fax: (206) 736-1501
Contact: Robert B. McCullough, President
Sales: Robert C. Pollock, VP Sales and Mktg.
Building Types: single-family, multi-family, commercial
Market Area: WA, OR, ID, MT, NV, AR, CA, AK, HI

GOLDEN WEST HOMES
1308 Wakeham
Santa Ana, CA 92705
(714) 835-4200, Fax: (714) 835-6232
Contact: Robert J. Henry, Sr. VP
Building Types: single-family
Market Area: CA, AZ, NV, HI, OR

Other Plant Locations:
South California Division
3100 N. Perris Blvd.
Perris, CA 92571
(714) 657-1611
Fax: (714) 943-9892
Contact: Phil Clark, Gen. Mgr.

Sacramento Division
9998 Old Placerville Road
Sacramento, CA 95827
(916) 363-2681
Fax: (916) 363-4587
Contact: Andy Karsten, Gen. Mgr.

Albany Division
2445 Pacific Blvd., South
Albany, OR 97321
(503) 926-8631
Fax: (503) 926-1251
Contact: Bruce Stoyer, VP Operations/Gen. Mgr.

GUERDON HOMES, INC.
Corporate Headquarters
5825 SW Meadows, Suite 315
Lake Oswego, OR 97035
(503) 624-6400
Fax: (503) 620-5929
Contact: Al Preusch, President
Sales: Bob Piantidosi, VP Marketing
Building Types: single-family
Market Area: South, Central, and West USA, Export

Other Plant Locations:
Magnolia Homes
Rt. 6 Box 33B, Hwy. 61S
Vicksburg, MS 39180
(601) 636-6455
Fax: (601) 636-0483
Contact: Howard McGrit, Gen. Mgr.

P.O. Box 657
982 Rondell Road
Gering, NE 69341
(800) 445-5423
Fax: (308) 436-3131
Contact: Roger Phillips, Operation Manager

1200 Wilco Road
Stayton, OR 97383
(503) 769-6333
Fax: (503) 769-6333
Contact: Curtis Richards, Gen. Mgr.

5556 Federal Way
Boise, ID 83706
(208) 345-5100
Fax: (208) 336-9629
Contact: Barry Rogers, Gen. Mgr.

HAVEN HOMES, INC.
P.O. Box 178
Route 150
Beech Creek, PA 16822
(717) 962-2111
(800) 543-7852
Fax: (717) 962-2965
Contact: Charles J. Mogish, CEO
Sales: Terry Peeler, Sales Manager
Building Types: single-family, multi-family, commercial
Market Area: Mid-Atlantic and New England

HECKAMAN HOMES
P.O. Box 229
26331 U.S. #6 East
Nappanee, IN 46550
(219) 773-4167
Fax: (219) 773-2546
Contact: Jerry Long, VP Marketing
Building Types: single-family, multi-family, condos
Market Area: MI, OH, IL, IN

HUNTINGTON HOMES, INC.
P.O. Box 98, Route 14
East Montepelier, VT 05651
(802) 479-3625, Fax: (802) 479-0689
Contact: Duane E. Webster, CEO
Building Types: single-family, multi-family, commercial
Market Area: New England and Eastern New York

Other Plant Locations:
Regional Sales Office
2 Bay Road
Hadley, MA 01035
(413) 584-9573
Contact: Larry Roux, Gen. Mgr.

INTEGRI HOMES
A Division of PLH Homes, Inc.
P.O. Box 491655
Leesburg, FL 34749-1655
(904) 787-2056, Fax: (904) 326-9003
Contact: Randy Shumate, VP/Gen. Mgr.
Sales: James R. Thomas, Sales Mgr.
Building Types: single-family, multi-family, commercial
Market Area: Florida

KAPLAN BUILDING SYSTEMS, INC.
Route 433 East
P.O. Box 247
Pine Grove, PA 17963
(717) 345-4635
(800) 527-6968
Fax: (717) 345-2642
Contact: Morris Kaplan, President
Sales: Paul Castle, Dir. Sales/Mktg.
Building Types: single-family, multi-family, commercial
Market Area: Northeast U.S.

Other Plant Locations:
Route 433 East
P.O. Box 247
Pine Grove, PA 17963
(717) 345-4635
(800) 527-6968
Fax: (717) 277-2642
Contact: Paul Castle, Dir. Sales and Mktg.

MILLER BUILDING SYSTEMS, INC.
P.O. Box 1283
Elkhart, IN 46515
(219) 295-1214
Fax: (219) 295-2232
Contact: John M. Davis, President/CEO
Sales: John F. Toboll, VP
  Rick Bedell, VP
Building Types: single-family, multi-family, commercial
Market Area: New England, Mid-Atlantic, Great Lakes,
  Plains, Northwest, CA, AK, HI

Other Plant Locations:
RR #4 Box 40
Sioux Falls, SD 57107
(605) 543-5399
Fax: (605) 543-5300
Contact: Dan Berdahl, Plant Manager

Western Division Headquarters
430 C Street
Patterson, CA 95363
(209) 892-6297
Fax: (209) 892-2599
Contact: Edward Bollero, President

58120 C.R. 3 South
P.O. Box 1283
Elkhart, IN 46515
(219) 295-1214
Fax: (219) 295-2232
Contact: Dennis Fredrickson, Plant Manager

Morse Road
P.O Box 528
Bennington, VT 05201
(802) 447-3541
Fax: (802) 442-3094
Contact: Scott Heckel, Plant Manager

2785 National Way
P.O. Box 40
Woodburn, OR 97971
(503) 981-1811
Fax: (503) 981-7732
Contact: Rob Podawiltz, Plant Manager

10225 Beech Avenue
P.O. Box 828
Fontana, CA 92335
(714) 350-3222
Fax: (714) 350-3910
Contact: Quentin Small, Plant Manager

64 Hess Road
P.O. Box 526
Leola, PA 17540
(717) 656-2081, Fax: (717) 656-6271
Contact: Rodney Young, Plant Manager

MITCHELL BROTHERS CONTRACTORS, INC.
960 Forestdale Blvd.
Birmingham, AL 35214
(205) 798-2020, Fax: (205) 674-5839
Contact: James E. Mitchell, President
Sales: Chris Matthews, Ron Braswell
Building Types: single-family, multi-family, commercial
Market Area: DE, MD, NC, OH, VA, WV, PA, KY, NJ

NRB INC. - MODULAR BUILDING SYSTEMS
115 S. Service Road
P.O. Box 129
Grimsby, Ontario L3M 4G3
(416) 945-9622, Fax: (416) 945-2003
Contact: Laurie Robert, Sales Mgr.
Building Types: commercial, special unit
Market Area: Canada

NANTICOKE HOMES, INC.
P.O. Box F
U.S. Route 13
Greenwood, DE 19950
(302) 349-4561, Fax: (302) 249-4561
Contact: John Mervine, President
Building Types: single-family, multi-family, commercial
Market Area: DE, MD, VA, PA, NJ

NATIONWIDE HOMES, INC.
P.O. Box 5511
100 Rives Road
Martinsville, VA 24115
(703) 632-7101
Fax: (703) 632-1181
Contact: Fredric J. Betz, President
Sales: Ronald C. Evans, VP Marketing
Building Types: single-family, multi-family, commercial
Market Area: Mid-Atlantic

NEW CENTURY HOMES/SIGNATURE BUILDING
    SYSTEMS
P.O. Box 9
1100 W. Lake Street
Topeka, IN 46571
(219) 593-2962
Fax: (219) 593-2044
Contact: Randy Meek, Gen. Mgr.
Sales: Tom Rusing, Sales Mgr.
Building Types: single-family, multi-family
Market Area: MI, IL, IN, OH, KY, WI, PA

NEW ENGLAND HOMES, INC.
270 Ocean Road
Greenland, NH 03840
(603) 436-8830
Fax: (603) 431-8540
Contact: Robert P. Killkelley
Building Types: single-family, multi-family, commercial
Market Area: ME, NH, VT, MA, CT, RI

NEWBERRY BUILDING SYSTEMS, INC.
P.O. Box 101
Newberry, MI 49868
(906) 293-8283
Fax: (906) 293-3322
Contact: John Slayter, President
Building Types: single-family
Market Area: Michigan

NORTH AMERICAN HOUSING CORP.
4011 Rock Hall Road
P.O. Box 145
Point of Rocks, MD 21777
(301) 694-9100
Fax: (301) 694-7570
Contact: Rodney Shapard, Exec. VP
Sales: Tim Reed, Dir. of Sales
Building Types: single-family, multi-family, commercial
Market Area: Eastern U.S.

Other Plant Locations:
P.O. Box 1279 Route 55 W
Front Royal, VA 22630
(703) 636-2991
Contact: Gary Bolt, Plant Manager

P.O. Box 25 State Road 684
Boones Mills, VA 24065
(703) 334-5000
Fax: (703) 334-5342
Contact: D. Lee Rankin, Gen. Mgr.

PENN LYON HOMES, INC.
Airport Road
P.O Box 27
Selinsgrove, PA 17870
(717) 374-4004, Fax: (717) 374-7429
Contact: Roger Lyons, President
Sales: Scott Schwartz, Sales Manager
Building Types: single-family, multi-family
Market Area: Northeast U.S., FL, MD, VA, Caribbean, Middle East

PRE-BUILT STRUCTURES, INC.
N. 5315 Corrigan Road
Otis Orchards, WA 99027
(509) 928-1442, Fax: (509) 928-7486
Contact: Eugene D. Zanck, President
Sales: Donald D. Moore (Consumers)
Perrin Zanck (Builders)
Building Types: single-family, multi-family, commercial, institutional
Market Area: WA, ID, OR, AK, HI, MT

PRINCETON HOMES CORPORATION
P.O. Box 2086
412 Princeton Road
Danville, VA 24541
(804) 797-3144, Fax: (804) 797-5645
Contact: Robert J. Jiranek, President
Sales: D.E. Scott, Jr., VP Marketing
Building Types: single-family, multi-family, commercial
Market Area: VA, NC, SC, WV

RANDAL COMPANY
Box 337
Piketon, OH 45661
(614) 289-4770
Contact: Emerson Leist
Sales: Craig R. Leist
Building Types: single-family
Market Area: OH, KY, WV

REGIONAL BUILDING SYSTEMS, INC.
5560 Sterrett Place
Suite 200
Columbia, MD 21044
(410) 997-7200
(800) 367-7512
Fax: (410) 995-5343
Contact: Edward C. Craig, President
Sales: Keith Sholos, VP
Building Types: single-family, multi-family, special projects
Market Area: Mid-Atlantic region

Other Plant Locations:
59 N. Leslie Road
North East, MD 21901
(301) 287-2700
Fax: (301) 575-6869
Contact: Keith Sholos, Plant Mgr.

#1 Joseph Mills Drive
Fredericksburg, VA 22401
(703) 371-6660
Fax: (703) 371-7127
Contact: Anna Vaught, Plant Mgr.

RITZ-CRAFT CORP. OF PA, INC.
P.O. Box 70
15 Industrial Park Road
Mifflinburg, PA 17844-0070
(717) 966-1053, Fax: (717) 966-9248
Contact: Kenneth L. Balliet, Dir. Special Projects
Sales: Paul D. John, Gen. Mgr.
Building Types: single-family, multi-family
Market Area: Northeast U.S., WV, MD, VA, DE

ROTEC INDUSTRIES
333 West Lake Street
Elmhurst, IL 60126
(708) 279-3300, Fax: (708) 279-3317
Contact: Robert Oury, President
Sales: John F. Mattson, Asst. Sales Mgr.
Building Types: pre-cut concrete modular housing
Market Area: worldwide

SCHULT HOMES CORPORATION
P.O. Box 219
Elkton, MD 21921
(301) 398-2100, Fax: (301) 398-6703
Contact: Warren Keyes, Jr., Gen. Mgr.
Building Types: single-family, multi-family
Market Area: Northeast and Mid-West U.S.

Other Plant Locations:
P.O. Box 151
Middlebury, IN 46540
(219) 825-5881
Contact: Dale Kase, Dir. of Mktg.

30 Industrial Park Road
Milton, PA 17847
(717) 742-8521
Contact: Dan Shields, Gen. Mgr.

P.O. Box 1218
437 North Main
Middlebury, IN 46540
(219) 825-7500
Contact: Don Swank, Gen. Mgr.

SCOTSMAN GROUP, INC., THE
8211 Town Center Drive
Baltimore, MD 21236
(410) 931-6000
Fax: (410) 931-6117
Contact: Barry Gossett, President
Building Types: commercial
Market Area: nationwide

Other Plant Locations:
P.O. Box 1169
Pierce Road
Winder, GA 30680
(404) 867-8040
Contact: Terry Bennett, Gen. Mgr.

201 West First Street
South Whitley, IN 46787
(219) 723-5131
Contact: David Preston, VP

18 Industrial Drive
North East, MD 21901
(301) 287-6300
2550 East 68th Street
Long Beach, CA 90805
(310) 531-0200
Contact: James Strode, VP

STRATFORD HOMES LTD. PARTNERSHIP
P.O. Box 37
Stratford, WI 54484
(715) 687-3113, Fax: (715) 687-3453
Contact: Glen Chadbourne, President
Sales: Russ Marti
Building Types: single-family, multi-family, commercial
Market Area: MN, WI, MI, IL, IA

TAYLOR HOMES
Highway 71 North
P.O. Box 438
Anderson, MO 64831
(417) 845-3311, Fax: (417) 845-6044
Contact: Clayton Meador
Sales: Kim Kerry, Mktg. Mgr.
Building Types: single-family
Market Area: AR, IL, IA, KS, MO, OK

TERRACE HOMES
301 South Main
P.O. Box 1040
Adams, WI 53910
(608) 339-7888, Fax: (608) 339-9714
Contact: Galen T. Manternach
Sales: Dave Kempfert
Building Types: single-, multi-family, commercial
Market Area: WI, MN, MI, IL, IA

U.S. HOUSING COMPONENTS, INC.
5890 Sawmill Road
Dublin, OH 43017
(614) 766-5101, Fax: (614) 766-6405
Contact: Frederick T. Forester, VP
Building Types: single-family, multi-family
Market Area: OH, IL, IN, KY, TN

Other Plant Locations:
3926 W. Highway 146
Buckner, KY 40010
(502) 222-1073
Contact: Steven W. Willis, President

UNIBILT INDUSTRIES, INC.
4671 Poplar Creek Road
P.O. Box 373
Vandalia, OH 45377
(513) 890-7570, Fax: (513) 890-8303
Contact: Douglas Scholz, President
Sales: Tom Shaw, Warner Bowling
Building Types: single-family
Market Area: OH, IN, KY, WV, MI

WAUSAU HOMES, INC.
P.O. Box 8005
Wassau, WI 54402-8005
(715) 359-7272, Fax: (715) 359-2867
Contact: Marvin Schuette, President
Building Types: single-family, multi-family, commercial
Market Area: WI, MN, IA, MI, IL, IN, OH, GA, NC, SC, FL

Other Plant Locations:
Hwy. 129 North Eatonton Hwy.
P.O. Box 1539
Gray, GA 31032
(912) 986-4590
Fax: (912) 986-4743
Contact: Rex Kennedy, Operations Mgr.

P.O Box 8005
Wausau, WI 54402-8005
(715) 359-7272
Contact: Frank Opatik

721 Alt. U.S. North
P.O. Box 308
Lake Wales, FL 33853
(813) 676-9390
Contact: Kirk Schoenburger, Division Mgr.

Advance Building Systems
750 West State Street
Charleston, IL 61920
(217) 345-3921
Contact: Tom Schuette, VP

Advance Building Systems
10854 Country Road, POB 327
Paulding, OH 45879
(419) 399-4412
Contact: Tom Schuette, VP

WESTCHESTER MODULAR HOMES, INC.
Reagan Mill Road
Wingdale, NY 12594
(914) 832-9400, Fax: (914) 832-6698
Contact: Steven Kerr
Building Types: single-family, multi-family, commercial
Market Area: New England, NY, NJ

4. Panelized Building Systems Council

The Panelized Building Systems Council is a national organization of manufacturers of pre-cut, panelized, and component building manufacturers. The following list includes the name and address of the manufacturer, phone number, and sales contact person. Contact individual manufacturers for information on design, floor plans and specifications, and builder/dealers in your area. The following list is provided by and courtesy of the Building Systems Councils of the National Association of Home Builders, 1201 15th Street, NW, Washington, DC 20005.

ALH BUILDING SYSTEMS
U.S. 224 West
P.O. Box 288
Markle, IN 46770
(219) 758-2141
Fax: (219) 758-2177
Contact: Kevin Cossairt, President
Sales: Maurice Cossairt
Building Types: single-family, multi-family, commercial
Market Area: worldwide

Other Plant Locations:
2933 E. 300 South
Huntington, IN 46750
(219) 758-2181
Contact: David Cossairt, VP

ACORN STRUCTURES
P.O. Box 1445
Concord, MA 01742
(508) 369-4111, Fax: (508) 371-1949
Contact: Arthur N. Milliken, President
Sales: Steven Stuntz, VP
Building Types: single-family, multi-family, commercial
Market Area: worldwide

ACTIVE HOMES CORPORATION
7938 South Van Dyke
Marlette, MI 48453
(517) 635-3532, Fax: (517) 635-3327
Contact: Alan Froehle, Exec. Director
Sales: Dick McHugh
Building Types: single-family, multi-family
Market Area: MI, worldwide

AMERICAN INGENUITY, INC.
3500 Harlock Road
Melbourne, FL 32934-8407
(407) 254-4220, Fax: (407) 254-9283
Contact: Glenda Busick, VP
Sales: Glenda Busick, Consumer Sales
Michael Busick, Builder Sales
Building Types: single-family, commercial
Market Area: U.S., Canada, Israel

AMOS WINTER HOMES
RR5, Box 168B
Glen Orne Drive
Brattleboro, VT 05301
(802) 254-3435, Fax: (802) 254-4999
Contact: Amos Winter, Owner
Sales: Pete Sanborn, Consumer Sales
Tom North, Builder Sales
Building Types: single-family, multi-family, commercial
Market Area: U.S., Canada, Europe, Mid and Far East

ARMSTRONG LUMBER CO., INC.
2709 Auburn Way N.
Auburn, WA 98002
(206) 852-5555, Fax: (206) 852-5556
Contact: James R. Armstrong, President
Sales: Jim DeSantis, Jeff Herlocker
Building Types: single-family, multi-family, commercial
Market Area: worldwide

AUTOMATED BUILDING SYSTEMS, INC.
309 Lafe Cox Drive
Johnson City, TN 37601
(615) 926-2158, Fax: (615) 926-4891
Contact: Brad Galbraith, VP
Building Types: single-family, multi-family, commercial
Market Area: worldwide

BARDEN & ROBESON CORP.
26 Copeland Avenue, P.O. Box 210
Homer, NY 13077
(607) 749-2641, Fax: (607) 749-3868
Contact: Edward Heselton, Head of Engineering
Sales: Robert Price, Sales Mgr.
Building Types: single-family, multi-family, commercial
Market Area: NY, NJ, NH, VT, MA, ME, PA, VA, MD, WV, CT

Other Plant Locations:
Kelly Ave.
Middleport, NY 14105
Contact: Robert Gelder, President

BLUE RIDGE TRUSS & SUPPLY, INC.
H.C. #65, Box 34
Bayse, VA 22810
(703) 856-2191
Fax: (703) 856-2908
Contact: Ted Watkins, Gen. Mgr.
Sales: Randy Thompson, International Sales Rep.
Building Types: floor and roof trusses, wall panels,
    single-family, multi-family, commercial
Market Area: MD, VA, WV, NC, PA

BRENTWOOD LOG HOMES
427 River Rock Blvd.
Murfreesboro, TN 37129
(615) 895-0720
Fax: (615) 893-4118
Contact: Tom Hogshead, President
Sales: Jim King, VP
Market Area: nationwide

BRISTYE, INC.
Box 818
Mexico, MO 65265
(314) 581-6663
Fax: (314) 581-5042
Contact: Gary A. Decker, President
Sales: Roy Overacre, Sales Mgr.
Building Types: single-family, multi-family, commercial
Market Area: MO, IA, KS, NE, IL, IN, AR, TN

CAROLINA BUILDERS CORPORATION
Panelized House Division
P.O. Box 58515
Raleigh, NC 27658
(919) 850-8270
Fax: (919) 850-8300
Contact: Dewey E. Alley, Mktg. Mgr.
Building Types: single-family, multi-family
Market Area: NC, SC, VA

CEDAR FOREST PRODUCTS COMPANY
107 W. Colden Street
Polo, IL 61064
(815) 946-3994, Fax: (815) 946-2479
Contact: Donald Much, President
Sales: Charles Monroe, Sales Engineer
Market Area: nationwide

CLASSIC POST & BEAM HOMES
Sales Model
P.O. Box 546
York, ME 03909
(207) 363-8210
(800) 872-BEAM
Fax: (207) 363-8210
Contact: Maggie Dustin
Building Types: single-family, multi-family, commercial
Market Area: worldwide

COASTAL STRUCTURES, INC.
P.O. Box 631, Laurence Road
Gorham Industrial Park
Gorham, ME 04038
(207) 854-3500
(800) 341-0300
Fax: (207) 854-0027
Contact: Thomas P. Drew, Operations Mgr.
Building Types: single-family, multi-family, commercial
Market Area: New England and Export

CRESTMANOR HOMES, INC.
P.O. Box 884
Martinsburg, WV 25401
(304) 267-4444, Fax: (304) 267-4139
Contact: Dan Sundahl, President
Building Types: single-family, multi-family, commercial
Market Area: worldwide

DELTEC HOMES
604 College Street
Asheville, NC 28801
(704) 253-0483, Fax: (704) 254-1880
Contact: Ken Crum, Exec. VP
Sales: Tim Alexander, Sales Mgr.
Building Types: single-family, multi-family, commercial
Market Area: worldwide

Other Plant Locations:
150 Westside Drive
Asheville, NC 28806
(704) 258-3685, Fax: (704) 254-2354
Contact: Charles Dacus, Production Mgr.

ENDURE-A-LIFETIME PRODUCTS, INC.
7500 NW 72nd Avenue
Miami, FL 33166
(305) 885-9901, Fax: (305) 888-6302
Contact: Jeffrey Kimmel, Chief Operations Officer
Building Types: single-family, multi-family, commercial
Market Area: Continental U.S.

FISCHER CORPORATION
1843 Northwestern Parkway
Louisville, KY 40203
(502) 778-5577
Fax: (502) 778-5581
Contact: Fred Fischer, President
Sales: J. Scott Brian
Building Types: single-family, multi-family, commercial
Market Area: worldwide

FOREST HOME SYSTEMS, INC.
RD#1, Box 131K
Selinsgrove, PA 17870
(717) 374-0131
(800) 872-1492
Fax: (717) 374-6093
Contact: John Garner, Sales Mgr.

GENTRY HOMES, LTD.
P.O. Box 295
Honolulu, HI 96809
(808) 671-6411
Fax: (808) 677-8855
Contact: Joseph J. Ramia, President
Building Types: single-family, multi-family, warehouses
Market Area: Hawaii

Other Plant Locations:
94-539 Puahi Street
Waipahu, HI 96797
(808) 671-6411
Contact: Jeffrey Brown, VP

HARVEST HOMES, INC.
1 Cole Road
Delanson, NY 12053-0189
(518) 895-2341
Fax: (518) 895-2287
Contact: Timothy O'Brien, CEO
Sales: Raymond Bohme, Joseph Messier
Building Types: single-family, multi-family
Market Area: NY, VT, MA, CT, NJ, NH, PA

HEARTHSTONE, INC.
Route 2, Box 434
Dandridge, TN 37725
(615) 397-9425
(800) 247-4442
Fax: (615) 397-9262
Contact: Randy Giles, President
Market Area: worldwide

K-K HOME MART, INC.
420 Curran Highway
North Adams, MA 01247
(413) 663-3765, Fax: (413) 663-9153
Contact: Ben Drew, Jr.
Building Types: single-family, multi-family, commercial
Market Area: New England and NY

KORWALL INDUSTRIES
326 North Bowen Road
Arlington, TX 76012
(817) 277-6741, Fax: (817) 265-9665
Contact: Stan Dimmick, President
Building Types: single-family, multi-family, commercial
Market Area: worldwide

LINDAL CEDAR HOMES
Box 24426
Seattle, WA 98124
(206) 725-0900, Fax: (206) 725-1615
Contact: Douglas Lindal
Building Types: single-family, commercial
Market Area: worldwide

MIRON BUILDING SYSTEMS, INC.
Center Street, Box 1538
Green Island, NY 12183
(518) 273-5473, Fax: (518) 273-5594
Contact: A.B. Clark, Mgr.
Sales: Buck Bovee
Building Types: single-family, multi-family, commercial
Market Area: NY, NJ, PA, CT, MA, VT, NH

NEW ENGLAND HOMES, INC.
270 Ocean Road
Greenland, NH 03840
(603) 436-8830, Fax: (603) 431-8540
Contact: Robert P. Killkelley
Building Types: single-family, multi-family, commercial
Market Area: ME, NH, VT, MA, CT, RI

NORTHERN COUNTIES HOMES
Rt. 50 West
P.O. Box 97
Upperville, VA 22176
(703) 592-3232, Fax: (703) 592-3552
Contact: Carl S. Hales, CEO
Sales: William Leachman, Tom Lyons, Tim Pasquerelli, John Stanford
Building Types: single-family, commercial
Market Area: VA, MD, WV, NC, PA, and Export

NORTHERN HOMES, INC.
51 Glenwood Ave.
Queensbury, NY 12804
(518) 798-6007
(800) 933-3931
Fax: (518) 798-3879
Contact: Michael Carusone, Chairman
Building Types: single-family, multi-family, light
 commercial
Market Area: U.S. and Export

REGIONAL BUILDING SYSTEMS, INC.
5560 Sterrett Place
Suite 200
Columbia, MD 21044
(410) 997-7200
(800) 367-7512
Fax: (410) 995-5343
Contact: Edward C. Craig, President
Sales: Keith Sholos, VP
Building Types: single-family, multi-family, special
 projects
Market Area: Mid-Atlantic region

Other Plant Locations:
59 N. Leslie Road
North East, MD 21901
(301) 287-2700
Fax: (301) 575-6869
Contact: Keith Sholos, Plant Manager

#1 Joseph Mills Drive
Fredericksburg, VA 22401
(703) 371-6660
Fax: (703) 371-7127
Contact: Anna Vaught, Plant Mgr.

RYLAND BUILDING SYSTEMS
10221 Wincopin Circle
Box 4000
Columbia, MD 21044
(301) 730-7222, (800) 367-7512
Fax: (301) 992-0455
Sales: Keith Scholos, VP Sales/Mktg.
International: Thurman Betz
Building Types: single-family, multi-family
Market Area: Continental U.S.

Other Plant Locations:
1310 Richey Road
Houston, TX 77073
(713) 443-4728
Contact: Dan Chaney, Plant Mgr.

11501 Ryland Court
Orlando, FL 32824
(407) 859-2166
Contact: Jeff Hollowell, Plant Mgr.

2312 Randolph Road
Shelby, NC 28150
(704) 482-5774
Contact: Jim Janda, Plant Mgr.

#1 Joseph Mills Road
Fredericksburg, VA 22401
(703) 371-6660
Contact: Rich Johnson, Plant Mgr.

6255 Kilby Road
Harrison, OH 45030
(513) 367-1718
1000 Tibbetts Lane
New Windsor, MD 21776-9097
(301) 549-1000
Contact: Lew Schwartz, Plant Mgr.

SACO HOMES
21 Timonium Road
Timonium, MD 21093
(301) 252-3030
(800) 695-SACO
Fax: (301) 252-6264
Contact: Carl D. Cherney, Operations Mgr.
Sales: Bill Edelen, VP Sales
Building Types: single-family, multi-family, commercial
Market Area: Mid-Atlantic states and Israel

SATTERWHITE LOG HOMES
Route 2, Box 256A
Longview, TX 75605
(903) 663-1729
(800) 777-7288
Fax: (214) 663-1721
Contact: Sam Satterwhite
Sales: Alan Hindman, Larry Bennett, Montly Stanley
Market Area: U.S., Japan, Mexico, Europe

Other Plant Locations:
4600 N. Stagecoach Road
Salado, TX 76571
(817) 947-8100
Contact: Jeff Alridge, Sales Representative

4600 Hwy. 6 West
Gypsum, CO 81637
(303) 524-7815
Contact: Randy Byrd, Timber Operations

SHELTER SYSTEMS CORPORATION
P.O. Box 830
633 Stone Chapel Road
Westminster, MD 21157
(301) 876-3900
Contact: Dwight Hikel
Sales: Joseph D. Hikel
Building Types: single-family, multi-family, commercial
Market Area: worldwide

Other Plant Locations:
Marne Highway
P.O. Box 450
Hainesport, NJ 08036
(609) 261-2000
Contact: Ed Maul, President

TIMBER TRUSS HOUSING SYSTEMS, INC.
525 McClelland Street
Salem, VA 24153
(703) 387-0273
Fax: (703) 389-0849
Contact: W.A. James, President
Building Types: single-family, multi-family, commercial
Market Area: Virginia and Export

TIMBERPEG
P.O. Box 474
West Lebanon, NH 03784
(603) 298-8820, Fax: (603) 298-5425
Contact: Adele Warner
Building Types: single-family, multi-family, commercial, post and beam
Market Area: U.S., Japan, Canada, Caribbean, England

Other Plant Locations:
P.O. Box 1500
Claremont, NH 03743
(603) 543-7762
Contact: Bob Britton

P.O. Box 70123
Reno, NV 89502
(702) 684-1722
Contact: Brenda Baldwin, Office Mgr.

P.O. Box 880
Fletcher, NC 28732
(704) 684-1722

P.O. Box 8988
Fort Collins, CO 80521
(303) 221-3355
Contact: Paul Bonazzoli, President

TOLL INTERNATIONAL, INC.
3103 Philmont Avenue
Huntington Valley, PA 19006
(215) 938-8000
Contact: Gideon Frishman, Director
Building Types: single-family, multi-family
Market Area: Israel

U.S. HOUSING COMPONENTS, INC.
5890 Sawmill Road
Dublin, OH 43017
(614) 766-5501
Fax: (614) 766-6405
Contact: Frederick T. Forester, VP
Building Types: single-family, multi-family
Market Area: OH, IL, IN, MI, KY, TN

UNIFIED CORPORATION
4844 Shannon Hill Road
Columbia, VA 23038
(804) 457-3622
(804) 556-6275
Fax: (804) 457-3649
Contact: David Mead, President
Building Types: single-family, multi-family, commercial
Market Area: worldwide

UNIHOME CORPORATION
Iron Horse Park
N. Billerica, MA 01862
(508) 663-6511
Fax: (508) 667-3290
Contact: Steven J. Mayo, Dir. of Sales and Mktg.
Building Types: single-family, multi-family, commercial
Market Area: nationwide

WAUSAU HOMES, INC.
P.O. Box 8005
Wassau, WI 54402-8005
(715) 359-7272
Fax: (715) 359-2867
Contact: Martin Schuette, President
Building Types: single-family, multi-family, commercial
Market Area: WI, MN, IA, MI, IL, IN, OH, GA, NC, SC, FL

Other Plant Locations:
Hwy. 129 North Eatonton Hwy.
P.O. Box 1539
Gray, GA 51032
(912) 986-4590, Fax: (912) 986-4743
Contact: Rex Kennedy, Operations Mgr.

P.O. Box 8005
Wausau, WI 54402-8005
(715) 359-7272
Contact: Frank Opatik

721 Alt. U.S. North
P.O Box 308
Lake Wales, FL 33853
(813) 676-9380
Fax: (813) 676-7961
Contact: Kirk Schoenburger, Division Mgr.

Advance Building Systems
10854 Country Road, POB 327
Paulding, OH 45879
(419) 399-4412
Fax: (419) 399-4361
Contact: Tom Schuette, VP

Advance Building Systems
750 West State Street
Charleston, IL 61920
(217) 345-3921
Fax: (217) 345-4024
Contact: Tom Schuette, VP

WESTCHESTER MODULUAR HOMES, INC.
Reagans Mill Road
Wingdale, NY 12594
(914) 832-9400
Fax: (914) 832-6698
Contact: Steven Kerr
Building Types: single-family, multi-family, commercial
Market Area: New England, NY, NJ

WOODLAND HOMES, INC.
P.O. Box 202
Lee, MA 02138
(413) 623-5739, Fax: (413) 623-5556
Contact: John Egee, President
Sales: Philip Dolan, VP
Market Area: New England and Eastern NY

WOODMASTER FOUNDATIONS, INC.
P.O. Box 66
845 Dexter Street
Prescott, WI 54021
(715) 262-3655, Fax: (715) 262-5079
Contact: Wayne Kimber, Jr.
Sales: Don Vogl, Consumer
Dwight Kimber, Builder Sales
Dan Krech, Builder Sales
Building Types: total wood foundations, earth-sheltered
 and wood earth-bermed homes
Market Area: East of the Rockies
Other Plant Locations:
P.O. Box 436
Carrollton, KY 41008
(502) 732-4427
Contact: Wayne Kimber, Jr.

YANKEE BARN HOMES, INC.
HCR 63, Box 2
Grantham, NH 03753
(603) 863-4545, (800) 258-9786
Fax: (603) 863-4551
Contact: Robert Knight, President
Building Types: single-family, commercial
Market Area: nationwide

Index

Value, factors affecting, cont.
    location, 75
    quality, 75
    size, 75
Veterans Administration, 68

W

Wall covering and molding, 63
Warranty, 60, 87

checklist, 87
    manufacturer's, 60
Wausau Homes, 92-100
    photos, 94-100
Westphal, Donald, 79
Windows, 57, 63

Z

Zoning, eliminating restrictions, 79